CW01668029

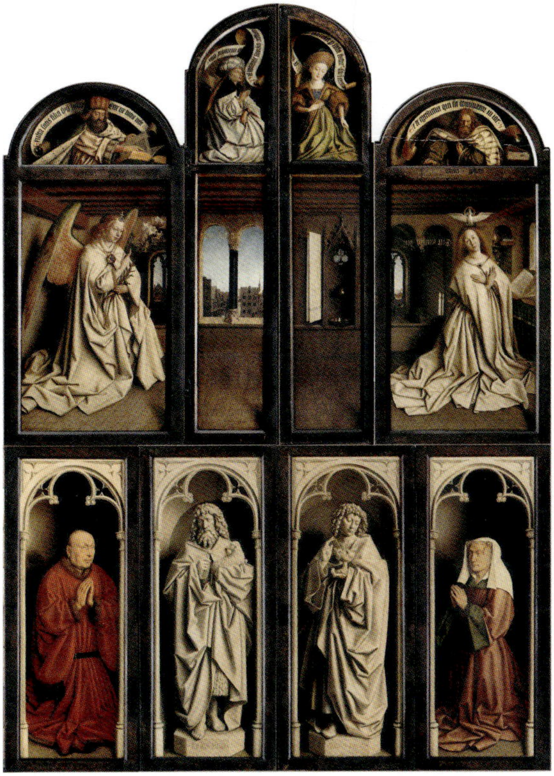

THE GHENT ALTARPIECE

Peter Schmidt

LUDION

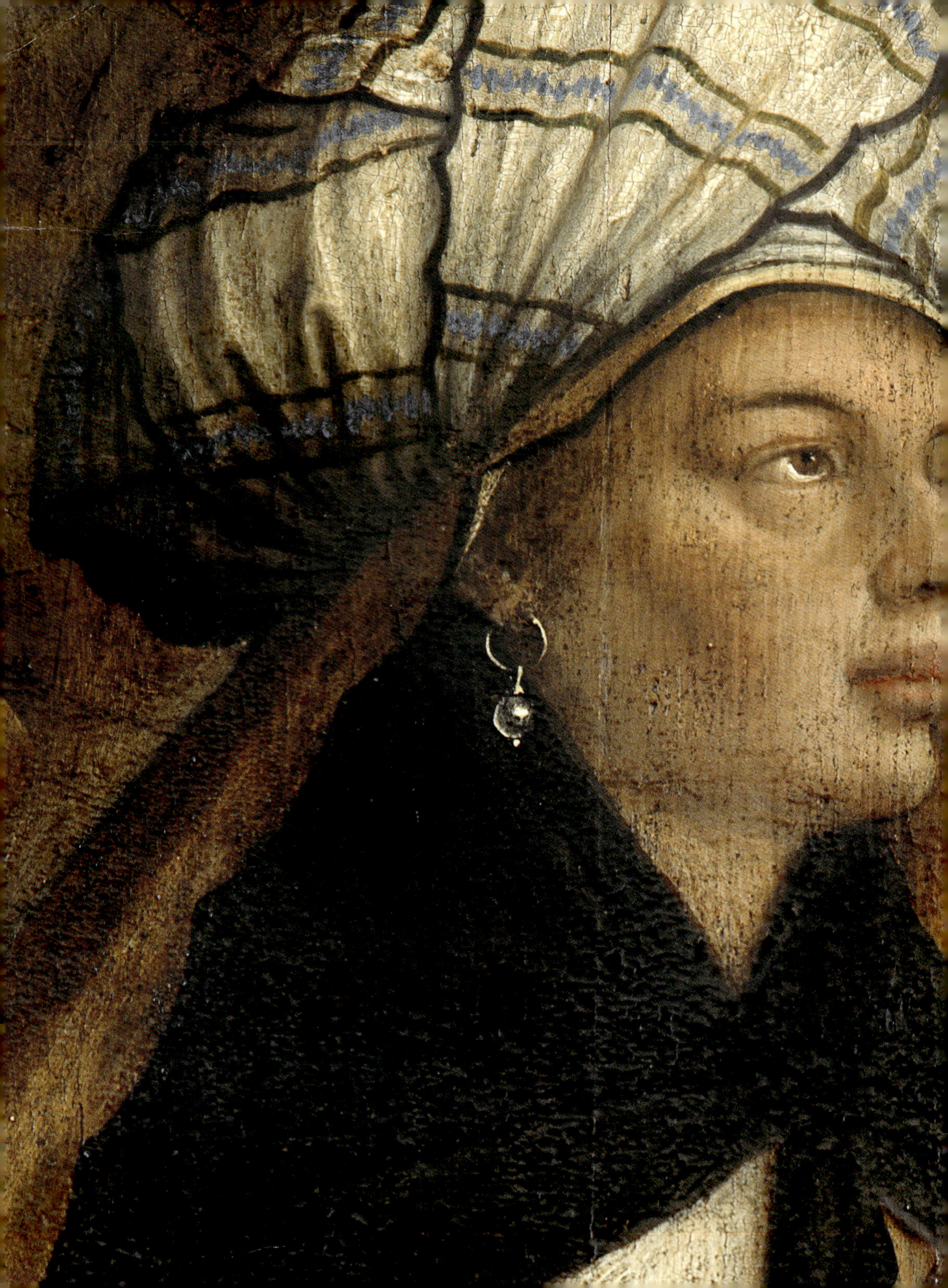

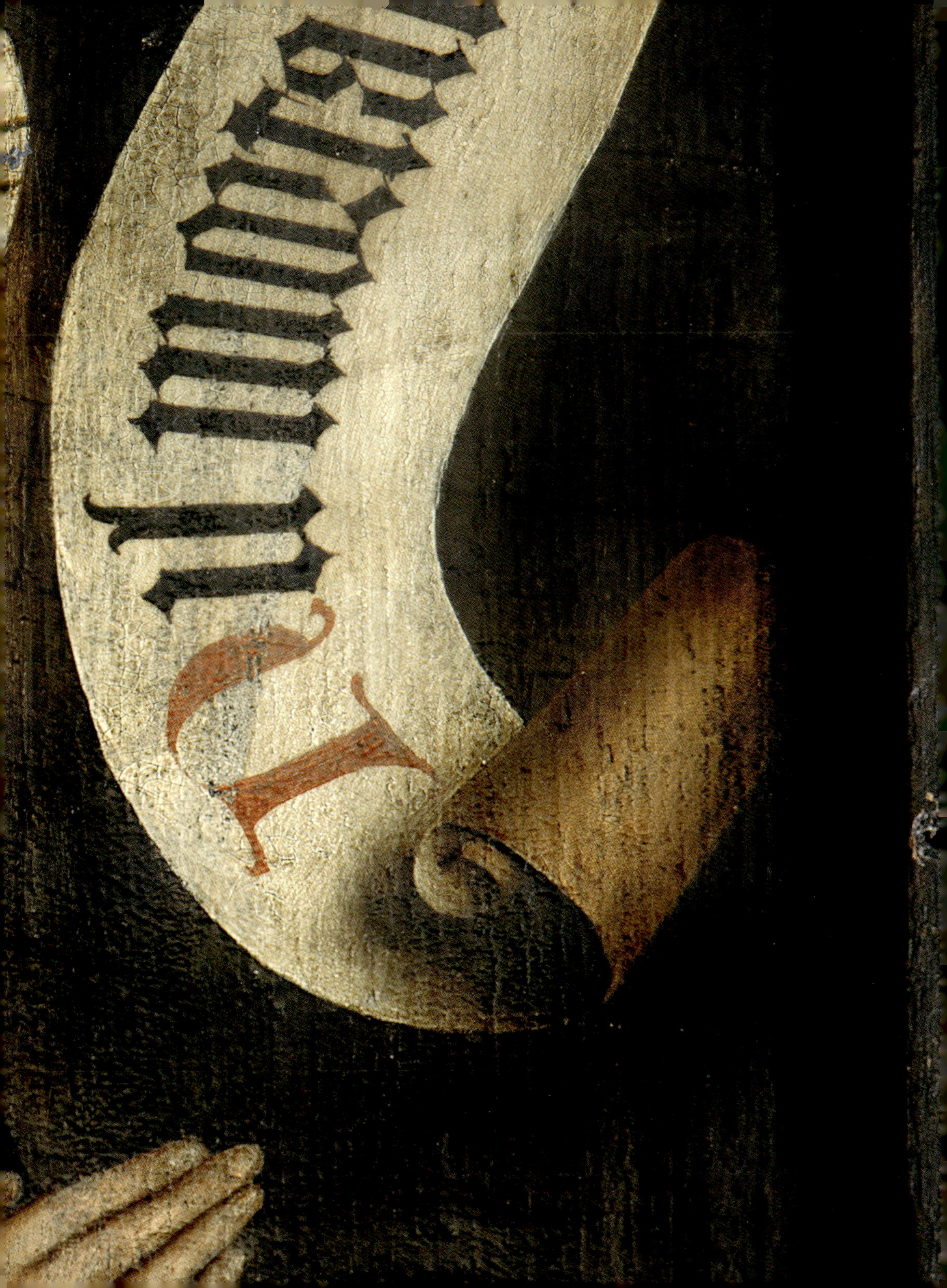

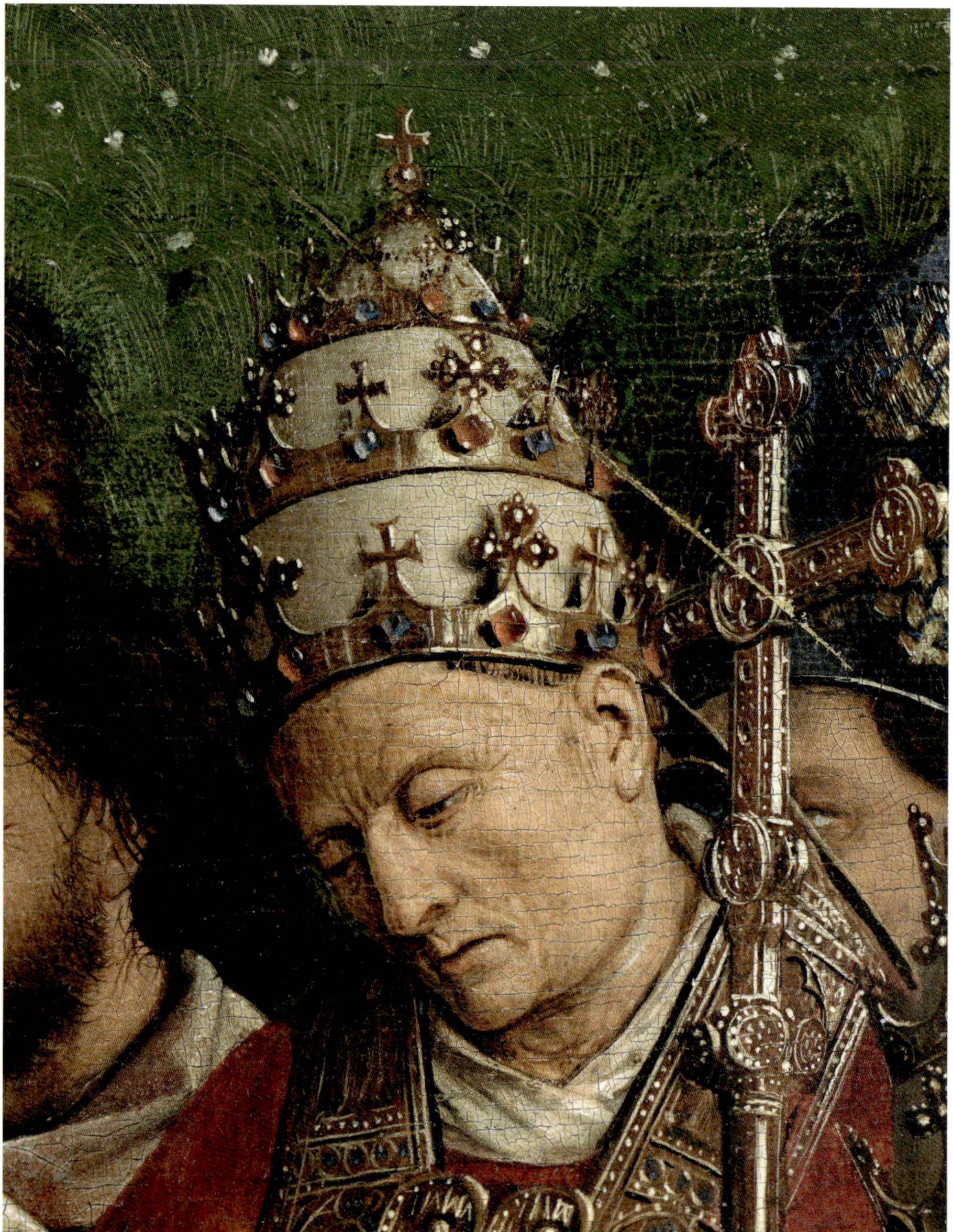

– 1 –

FLANDERS AT THE TIME OF VAN EYCK

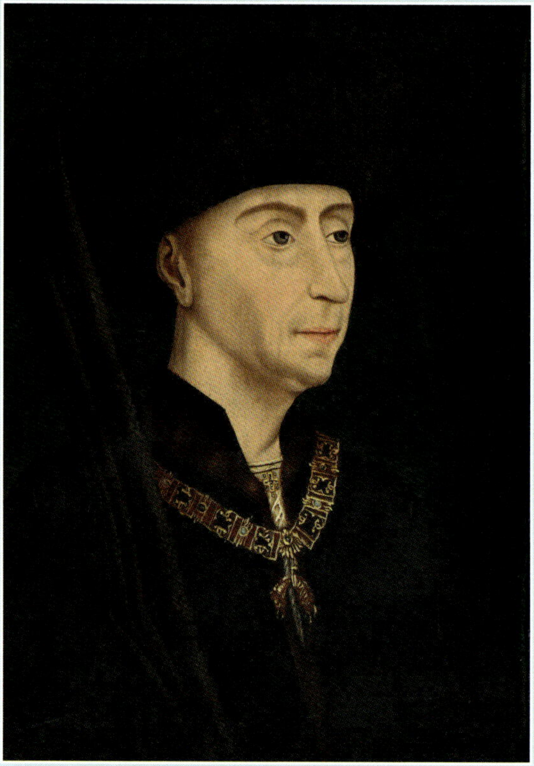

After Rogier van der Weyden,
Portrait of Philip the Good, Duke of Burgundy,
15th century

Duke Philip III of Burgundy succeeded to his title in 1419, heralding in a period of immense economic and cultural affluence throughout his territories, which ran from Franche-Comté to Frisia. Little surprise, then, that he was nicknamed 'Philip the Good'. He began his long reign (1419–67) with a passing involvement in the Hundred Years War between England and France, which dragged on until 1453. He also maintained a fleet against the Ottoman Empire and was very much a crusader at heart. At home, however, he presided over an extended peace, which encouraged the economic flowering of his territories, the two richest of which were Burgundy and the County of Flanders. The latter, which boasted the glittering commercial cities of Bruges, Ghent and Ypres, gave the region a pivotal role in the European economy. In 1425 – six years after assuming his inheritance – Philip was involved in the foundation of the new university at Leuven (Louvain), which was destined to become the intellectual Mecca of his region. The Duke was not only a brilliant politician and diplomat, he was also a generous patron of the arts.

He created the Order of the Golden Fleece in 1430, transformed the appearance of his capital city of Dijon – not to mention other cities – and provided work to countless craftsmen, artists and musicians throughout his territories. Some of the greatest figures of the age worked directly for Philip and his court. If we consider that Jan van Eyck lived between around 1385 and 1441, that Rogier van der Weyden died in 1464 and Dieric Bouts in 1475, it is plain that the first great efflorescence of the 'Flemish Primitives' coincided with the period of Philip the Good's rule.

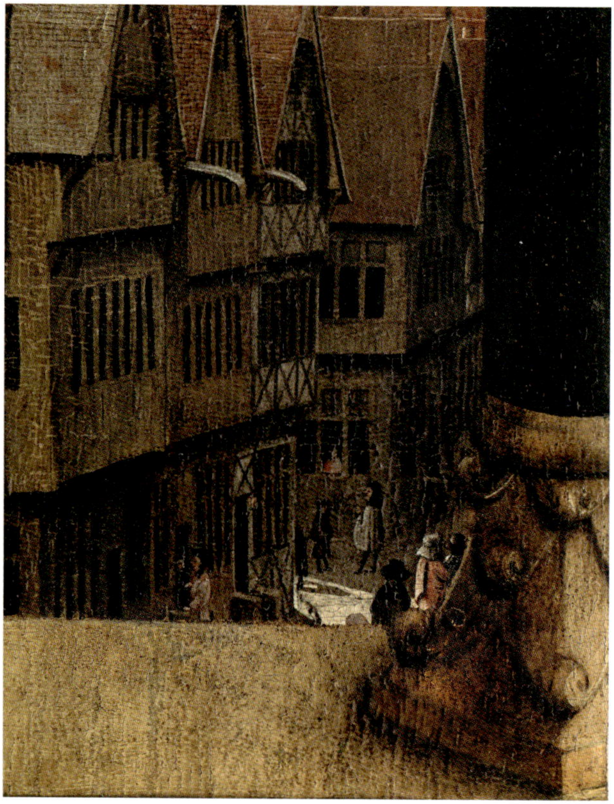

The burgher class in the major cities benefited immensely from the prestige of Philip's rule. Although poverty remained rife, the relative standard of living in the leading centres of the Burgundian empire was high. The burghers of Bruges and Ghent grew rich from commerce, enabling them to develop a highly genteel lifestyle. The principal business in Ghent was the flourishing cloth trade – one of the largest sources of income in the County's leading city since the Middle Ages. The wealth and importance of Ghent's citizens – or poorters – is apparent from the fact that they too were able to commission important works of art, alongside the secular and religious potentates who were the artists' more traditional patrons. This is the context in which we have to examine the creation of the Adoration of the Lamb. The altarpiece was not produced as a gift to or commission from a prince, but through the patronage of prominent citizens.

View of Medieval Ghent (Kortedagsteeg)

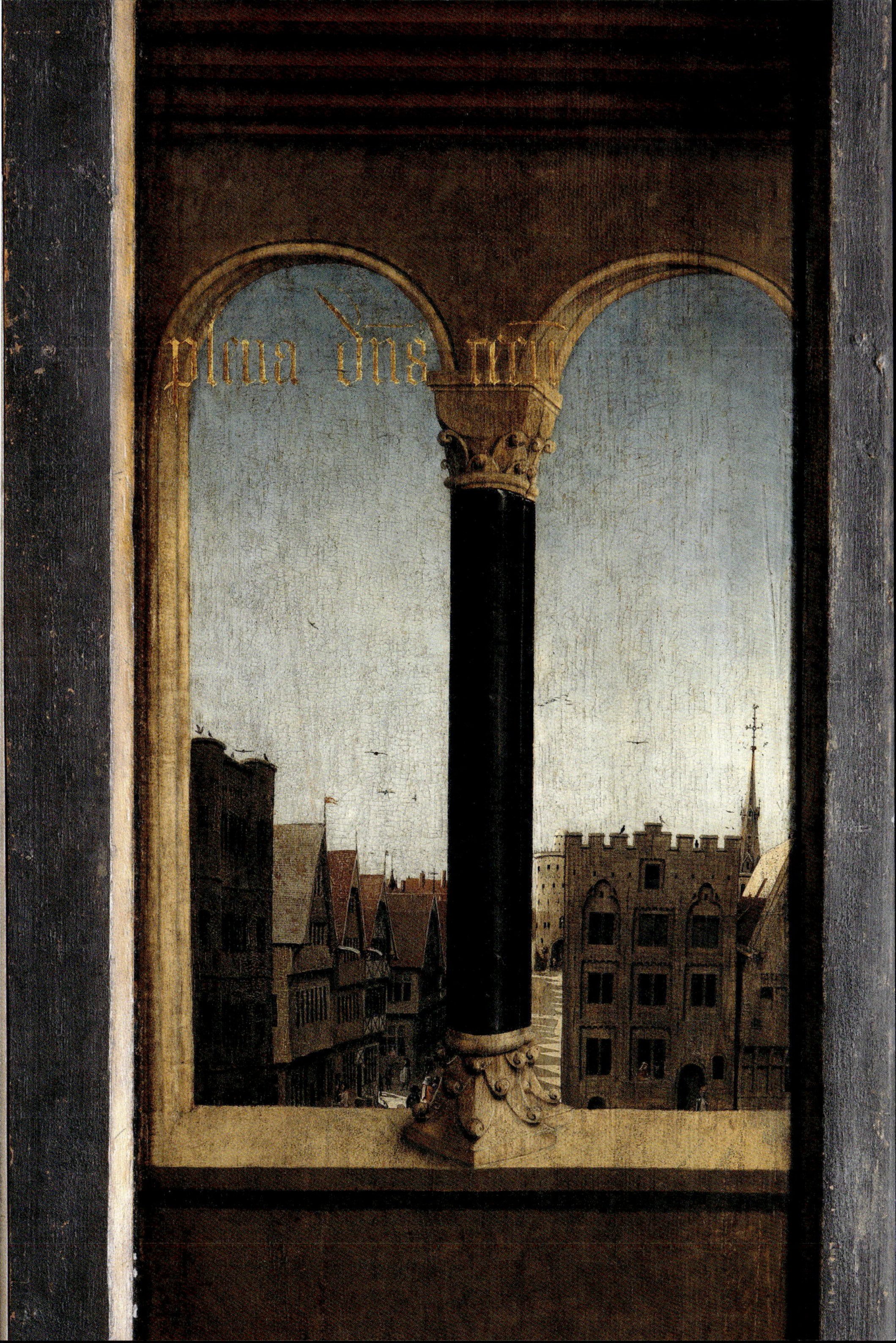

– 2 –

THE PARISH OF ST JOHN – A CHURCH IN GHENT

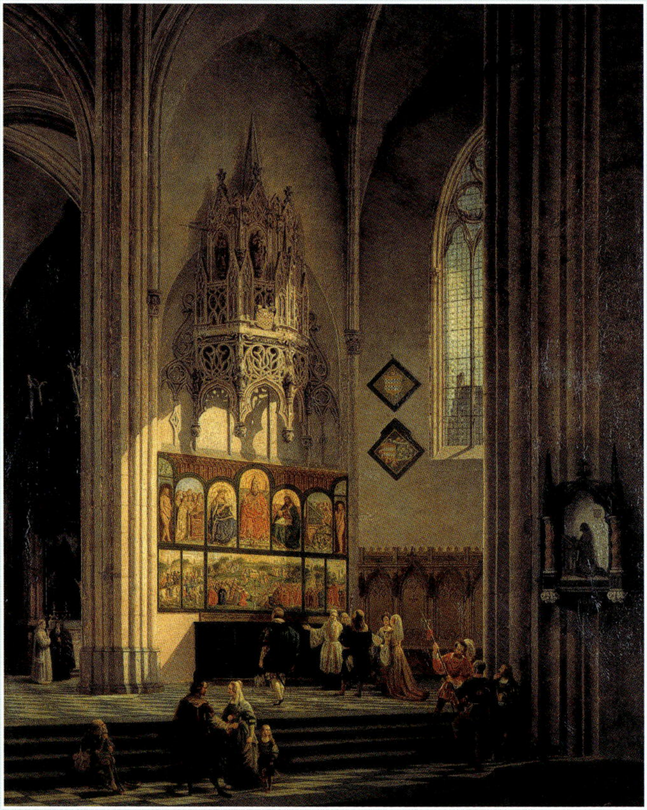

Pieter Frans de Noter and Felix de Vigne,
Albrecht Dürer Admires the Ghent Altarpiece by Jan and Hubert van Eyck, 1840

What is now the Cathedral of St Bavo, was originally the parish church of St John the Baptist. It was the oldest church within the city walls, while the parish of St John was Ghent's earliest independent parish – also by far its most prestigious. It was home to many wealthy and prominent citizens, a fact reflected in the scale of the building and the splendour of its interior. The Counts of Flanders and other powerful figures consistently chose the church as the setting for important ceremonial events. Whenever the region's rulers gave money for church buildings and interiors, St John's was at the top of the list of beneficiaries. All the same, the church was largely built with money raised within the parish itself – one of the reasons for the extremely long duration of its construction. The Gothic choir was the only part of the current building to have been completed in the period when Van Eyck was active. The transept and nave were still Romanesque – survivals from the stone church built on the site in the 12th century. Rich parishioners were only too happy to contribute to the interior of the church. At the height of the Middle Ages, it was primarily the guilds that fulfilled this role, but in the Burgundian period, when Flanders developed a wealthy burgher class, the number of individual donors for parts of the building and works of art increased. Jodocus Vyd and his wife Elizabeth Borluut were among the church's parishioners and it was in this context that they donated an altarpiece to the chapel that bears Vyd's name to this day.

Ghent's cathedral has only been known as St Bavo's since 1540. The latter proved to be a year of intense humiliation for the local population, with Emperor Charles V returning in person to punish his native city for its far-reaching resistance to taxes he had imposed to finance his military campaigns. Charles abolished the city's medieval privileges, imposed his 'Concession' on it, forced the City Council to beg for his forgiveness, and had a number of rebels walk in procession past his judge's seat, dressed in their shirts and with nooses around their necks. People of Ghent have been known as *stroppendragers* ('noose-wearers') ever since. And still Charles was not satisfied. He demolished several city gates and installed a Spanish garrison in the city. He climbed the new tower of the principal church to pick out a strategically suitable spot, opting for the site occupied by the prestigious and centuries-old Abbey of St Bavo. The pleas of the City Council and the abbey itself were to no avail. St Bavo's was to be demolished to make way for a fortress, which was known as the 'Spaniards' Castle'. He gave permission to the monks, who had become secular in 1536–37, to move their chapter to the Church of St John. The latter, a parish church, subsequently adopted the name of the former abbey. Despite this, the cathedral crypt is still dedicated to St John the Baptist. A few years later, at the height of the conflict with the Protestants, King Philip II asked the Pope to reorganise the various dioceses in the Low Countries, which had grown too large and unmanageable. Fourteen new bishoprics were duly founded on 12 May 1559. The ones in Flanders were Mechelen (Malines), Antwerp, Ypres, Bruges and Ghent. The Church of St Bavo was selected as the bishop's seat in Ghent, earning it promotion to cathedral status.

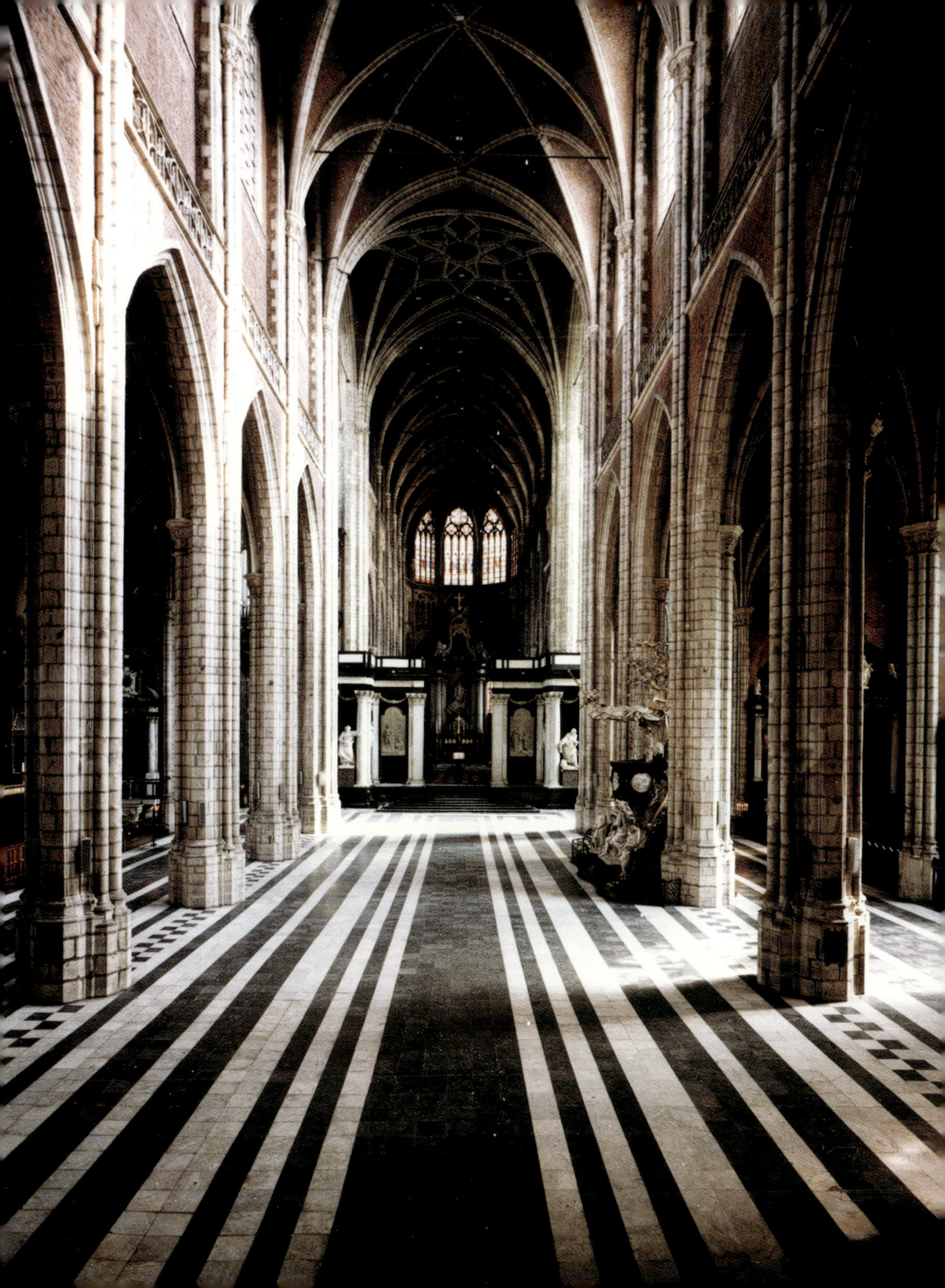

– 3 –

THE PATRONS AND DONORS

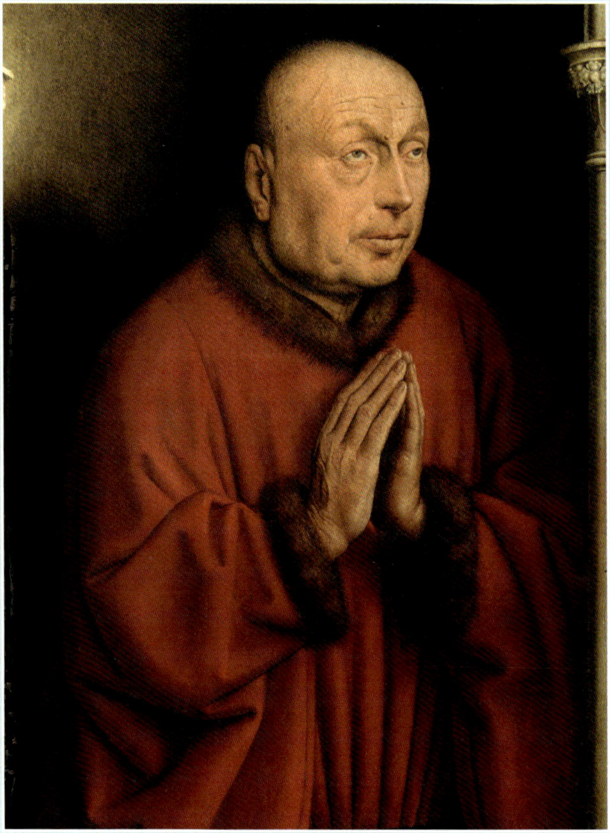

Jodocus Vyd

Jodocus (Joos) Vyd, Lord of Pamele, belonged to an extremely wealthy family of financiers. He was one of the leading citizens of Ghent and was involved in the city's administration for many years. In 1433–34, he became First Alderman – more or less equivalent to the modern post of burgomaster or mayor. His wife Elizabeth (Isabella) was a Borluut – one of the city's most important historical families. The Borluuts' former mansion can still be seen on Korenmarkt, whereas all that remains of Vyd's house are the extensive Gothic cellars below a building in what is now Gouvernementstraat. Vyd himself was a parishioner of St John's and helped finance the restoration of one of the radiating chapels in the Church of St John between 1410 and 1420. It is known as the 'Vyd Chapel' in his honour. To mark the inauguration of the chapel, Vyd and his wife decided to commission a costly altarpiece. They did so by endowing a foundation – a common ecclesiastical practice whereby a churchgoer would provide the funds to pay for a particular ritual that was to be carried on at regular intervals in the future. In the case of the Adoration of the Lamb, this took the form of a daily Mass 'In honour of God, His Blessed Mother and All His Saints'. The foundation was intended to contribute to the salvation of the donors and their forebears.

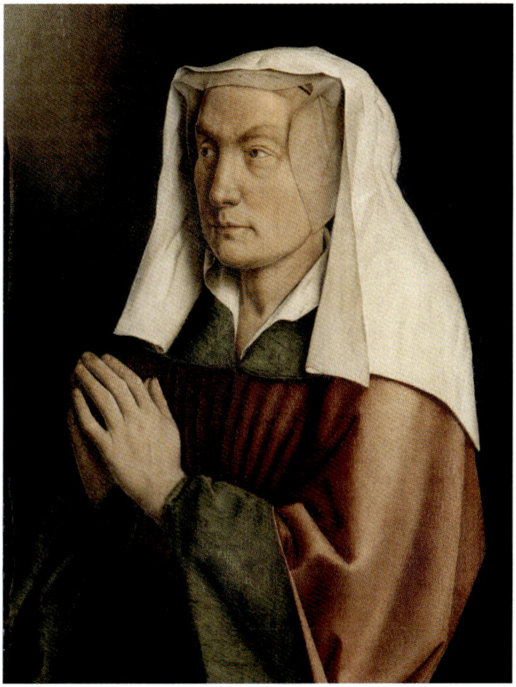

Elizabeth Borluut

THE SIGNIFICANCE OF CHRIST AS THE LAMB OF GOD

The foundation of a Mass was perfectly in keeping with the Lamb of God theme. Christ, represented as a lamb, is a frequent motif in Eucharistic symbolism. Countless communion rails and liturgical objects (chalices, copes and so on) are decorated with the Lamb of God. The meaning is clear to anyone familiar with Christian symbolism. Christ is first referred to as the 'Lamb of God' in the Gospel of St John (1:35), where the words are spoken by the other St John – the Baptist.

The significance of Jesus Christ as the Lamb of God can be traced to several sources. The first is the paschal lamb. According to the Bible (Exodus 12), the Jewish ritual of the paschal lamb was instituted by Moses on the Israelites' liberation from slavery in Egypt. During the annual Jewish celebration of the Passover, the eating of the paschal lamb recalled the salvation of Israel. It evolved into a symbol of the desired liberation from all forms of oppression and misery. Christians believed that Christ's death on the cross represented redemption from evil. Jesus' death and subsequent resurrection thus became the key Christian festival of Easter and the ultimate Paschal Feast. The association of the Crucifixion with the slaughter of the paschal lamb was an obvious next step. The notion was expressed at an early stage by the Apostle Paul, who wrote, 'Our paschal lamb, Christ, has been sacrificed' (I Corinthians 5:7). According to John's Gospel, Jesus died in the afternoon of the Day of Preparation – in other words, the moment when the paschal lambs were being slaughtered in the Temple. As with those lambs (Exodus 12:46), 'None of his bones shall be broken' (John 19:36). In the Gospel of St John and thereafter in Christian tradition, Jesus thus came to be identified as the true paschal lamb – humanity's redeemer.

A second association with the Lamb can be found in the prophets Isaiah and Jeremiah: *the servant of God is led like a lamb to the slaughter, helpless and dumb in the face of his executioners* (Isaiah 53:7; Jeremiah 11:19). This image too was interpreted at an early stage of the Christian tradition as a reference to the Passion of Christ.

The third idea is woven in golden letters into the antependium of the altar shown in the painting: ECCE AGNUS DEI QUI TOLLIT PECCATA MUNDI (Behold the Lamb of God, who will take away the sins of the world) – the words that John the Baptist spoke of Jesus (John 1:29). They are still intoned three times during every Mass. The allusion is to the ritual of the scapegoat, which, on the Day of Atonement (Yom Kippur), was symbolically laden with all the sins of Israel and banished into the wilderness (Leviticus 16:20–22). The scapegoat theme was transposed in the New Testament to that of redemption through the Lamb of God. By sacrificing his life, Jesus took away all the sins of the world. Each of these three meanings is profoundly linked to the symbolism of the Eucharist and the idea of humanity's salvation through Christ's sacrifice. Together they form the overarching theme of Van Eyck's altarpiece.

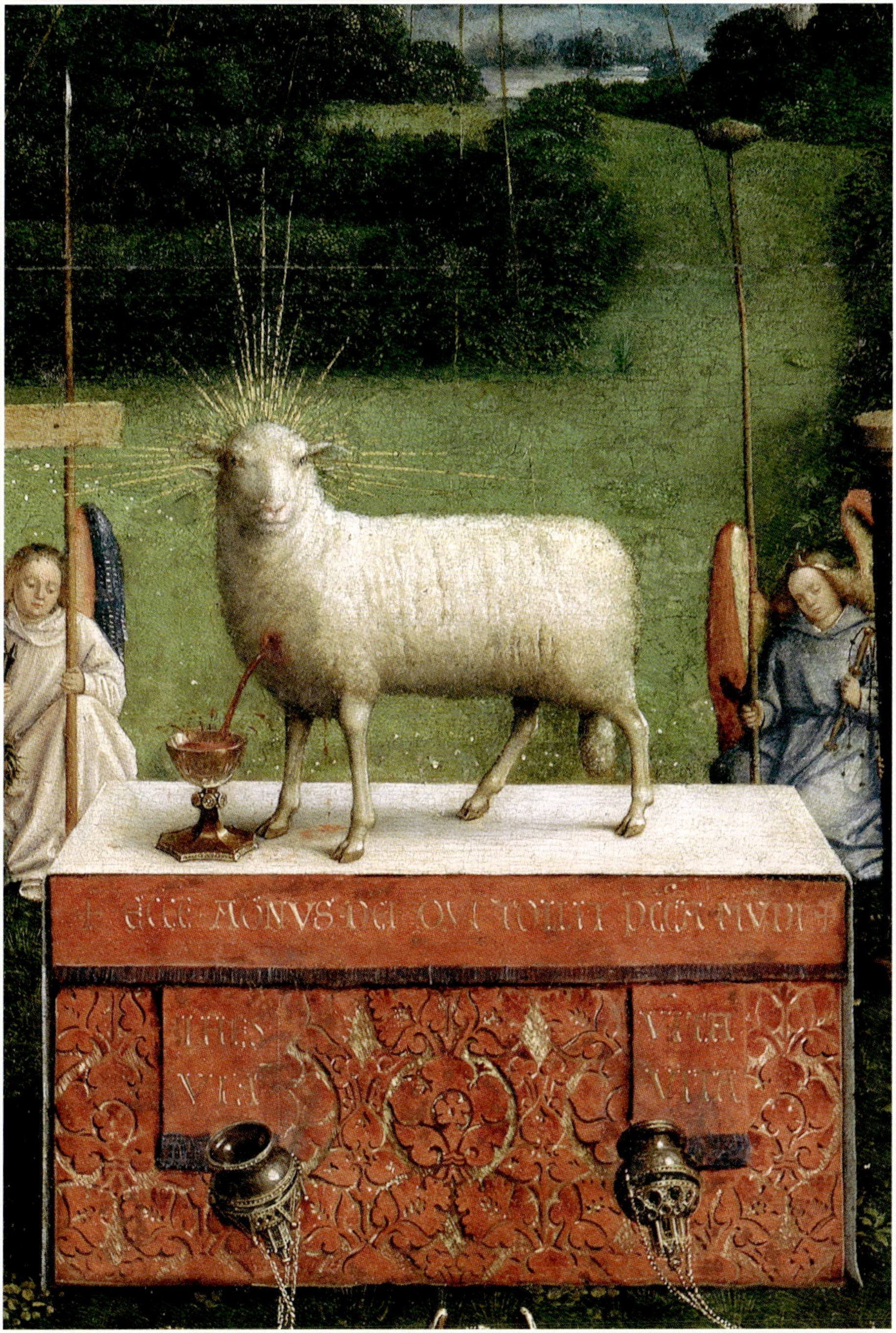

17-

– 4 –

THE PAINTERS

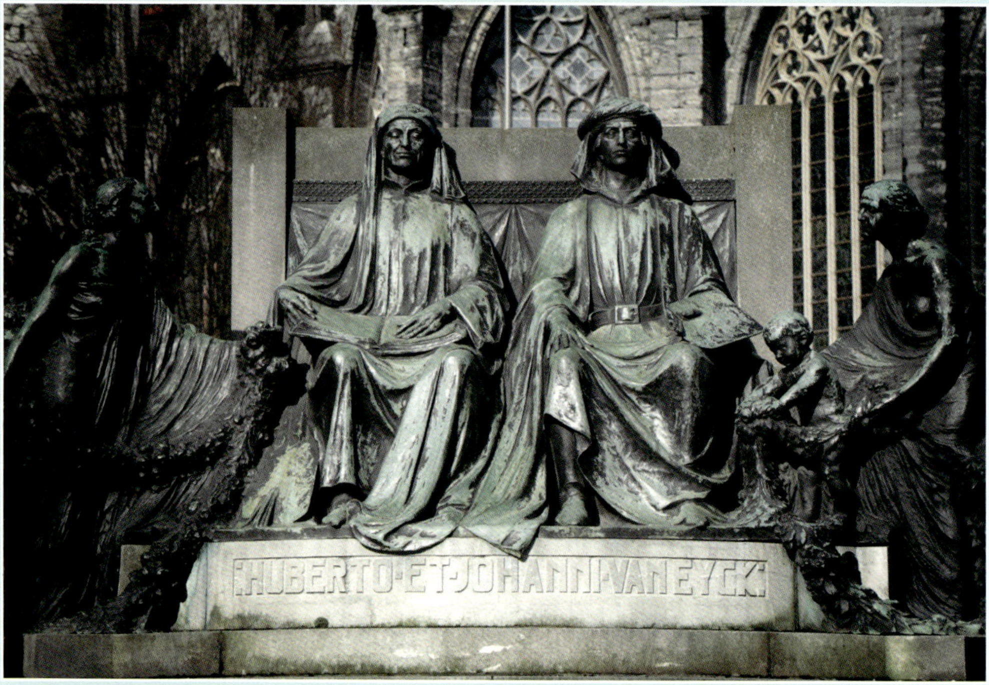

Monument to the Van Eyck brothers,
south-east of the cathedral of Saint Bavo

The Van Eyck brothers belonged to a family of painters in Limburg – probably Maaseik. Jan van Eyck (c. 1385–90 – Bruges 1441) is by far the best-known member of the family on account of his surviving work – he was the only one to leave behind signed and dated paintings, or ones that can be firmly attributed to him. The *Madonna of Canon van der Paele*, the *Portrait of Giovanni Arnolfini and his Wife* and several other portraits are all numbered among the greatest masterpieces of the museums fortunate enough to possess them. Although all of Jan van Eyck's surviving paintings were done in the final decade of his life, they are still the earliest dated works in early Netherlandish painting. His dazzling talent and intellectual brilliance evidently brought Jan to the attention of Duke Philip the Good. He worked for many years as Philip's court painter and also performed several sensitive diplomatic missions on the Duke's behalf. Relations between the two must have been excellent, as Philip even agreed to act as godfather to one of Van Eyck's sons. Although we are more or less certain that Jan van Eyck was the author of eighteen panels – nine of which are signed – his precise contribution to the Ghent Altarpiece has yet to be satisfactorily determined. A four-line Latin verse on the polyptych's frame states that the painting was commenced by Jan's elder brother (c. 1360–70 – Ghent 1426). The quatrain is extremely complimentary about Hubert, calling him the greatest painter there was. Jan – 'second in art' – is said to have completed the altarpiece at the urging of Jodocus Vyd. No other work by Hubert has been identified, at least not with any certainty. The art-historical void around him is so complete that his very existence was questioned at one stage. Municipal accounts and a tombstone in the refectory of the Abbey of St Bavo confirm, however, that Hubert was real enough. The praise expressed by the quatrain would be incomprehensible, if we did not accept that Hubert conceived and executed a substantial proportion of the altarpiece. It is thought that Vyd must have commissioned the work around 1420. Hubert then supposedly worked on it for five or six years until his death in 1426. Jan was involved in diplomatic business for the Duke around this time, and is unlikely to have been able to start work on the altarpiece until 1430 or afterwards. It seems likely, therefore, that he completed the painting between 1430 and 6 May 1432 – the date on which it was installed in the Vyd Chapel. Which of the two artists painted which parts of the altarpiece is an issue that has not been settled after almost 600 years. Owing to the extremely even distribution of paint, it is impossible to separate the painters' hands. Recent studies have tended to attribute the flatter, more two-dimensional figures – the three central figures, for instance, and those of the musical angels in the wings – to Hubert. Hubert must also have largely conceived the design of the altarpiece, although the theological aspect will have been developed in consultation with a theologian. Many scholars believe that the then parish priest of St John's, the highly learned Johannes van Impe, fulfilled this role. However, monks from St Bavo's Cathedral or St Peter's Abbey in Ghent might also have provided theological advice.

We may well have to look vertically rather than horizontally when seeking to distinguish Hubert's contribution from Jan's. In other words, the relationship between unfinished and finished may not lie so much in the visible surface as in the layers of paint below it. As with most paintings of its time, the Adoration of the Lamb was painted on oak panels roughly one centimetre thick. A hard, ivory-coloured base layer, comprising an emulsion of chalk powder and glue (gesso), was first applied to the wood. The artist then used this as the support for the underdrawing, in which he set down the outlines of the figures. Hubert may have completed this process for the whole of the inside of the altarpiece, with the exception of Adam and Eve, who are generally ascribed to Jan alone. The work was then built up through the application of several thin layers of paint on top of one another. Each layer allows different frequencies of light to pass through and reflects others, which explains the extraordinary luminosity of the colours. It may be, therefore, that the underdrawing had been completed by the time of Hubert's death, together with the first and second layers of paint in certain areas, and all the layers in others. It is also possible, however, that Jan painted the finishing layers on top of his elder brother's work, in which case we have to seek Hubert's hand not alongside Jan's but beneath it. Whatever the case, some of the earlier designs were certainly altered during the painting process. X-ray photographs show, for instance, that the Mediterranean vegetation in the panels with the hermits and pilgrims conceals what were originally more indigenous-looking trees.

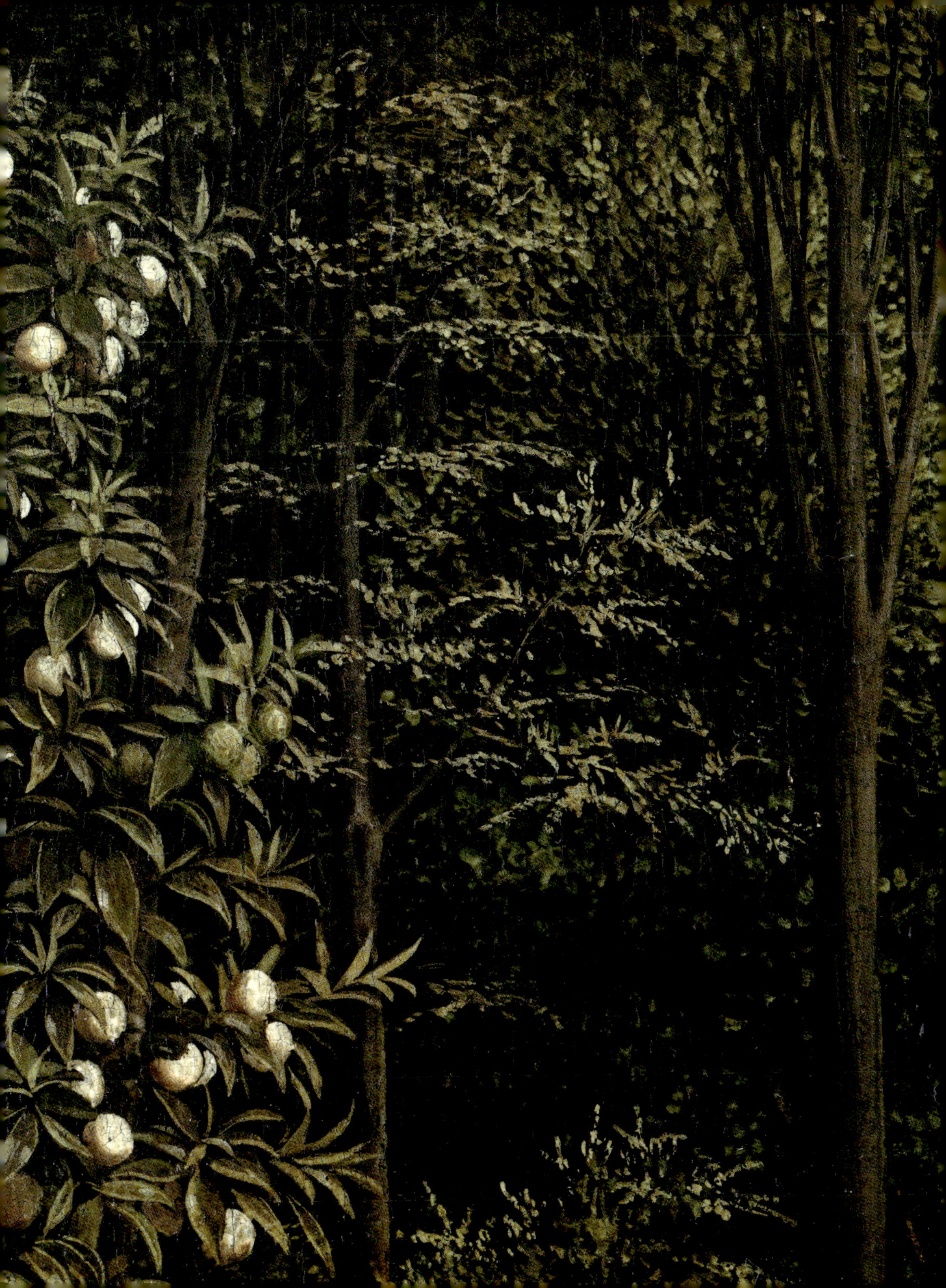

BRIEF HISTORY OF THE ALTARPIECE

Although its fine state of preservation might suggest otherwise, the Ghent Altarpiece has led anything but a peaceful existence. It had to be hidden from iconoclasts in both 1566 and 1578, during the religious troubles between Catholics and Protestants. It was also cleaned several times before 1700, during which minor restoration was performed.

Its true adventures only began, however, at the time of the French Revolution. In 1794, during the French occupation of Flanders, the four central panels of the altarpiece were taken to Paris, where they remained until the defeat of Napoleon at Waterloo in 1815. They were then returned, but in 1816, Ghent's Grand Vicar Le Surre sold the wings – though not Adam and Eve – to the Brussels antiquarian L.J. Nieuwenhuys for 6000 francs. The latter re-sold them a year later for 100,000 francs to the English collector E. Solly, who was residing at the time in Aachen. Solly's entire collection was then sold for 500,000 thalers to King Friedrich-Wilhelm III of Prussia in 1821. The paintings remained in the museum in Berlin until 1918. During that time, the panels were sawn apart to separate the front from the back, and cradled for an exhibition in 1894.

A fire in the Vyd Chapel in 1822 came close to destroying the remaining central panels. Hot ash fell on the altarpiece, and, as rescuers hurriedly sought to remove it from the flames, the large panel with the Adoration of the Lamb broke in two across the middle. The split can still be seen running through the bushes above the lamb. When the panel was restored, part of the lawn in the background, as well as the lamb itself, had to be overpainted. The traces of this can still be made out – the legs are all that remain of Van Eyck's original lamb. The Belgian State bought the Adam and Eve panels in 1861 and moved them to Brussels. In exchange, six copies by Michiel Coxcie were given to the church, and Victor Lagye painted new panels in which the first couple is shown demurely clothed. By this stage, the original ensemble had been significantly disfigured.

The dismantled altarpiece was not reunited until 1918. Under the terms of the Treaty of Versailles, the Germans handed back the panels from Berlin, in return for which the sum of 75,000,000 francs was deducted from the outstanding sum of war reparations. At the same time, the State returned the Adam and Eve panels, thus bringing the entire altarpiece back together for the first time since 1794. Reunification was to prove short-lived. On the night of 10–11 April 1934, the panel containing the Just Judges on one side and John the Baptist on the other was stolen. The thief, whose ransom demands to the diocese were signed with the initials d.u.a., returned the grisaille of the saint via the left-luggage office of Brussels North Station, but held on to the Just Judges, in the hope of extorting a large sum of money. The story took a new twist when the probable thief – Arsène Goedertier – died unexpectedly that same year. He confessed on his deathbed that he knew where the panel was located, but in spite of all manner of searches in the ensuing decades – some more plausible than others – the lost treasure has never been found.

The altarpiece's vicissitudes did not end in 1934. On 16 May 1940, the panels were transported to the castle of King Henri IV of France in Pau, to keep them from falling into German hands. However, the Nazis pressurised the Vichy government, which sent the

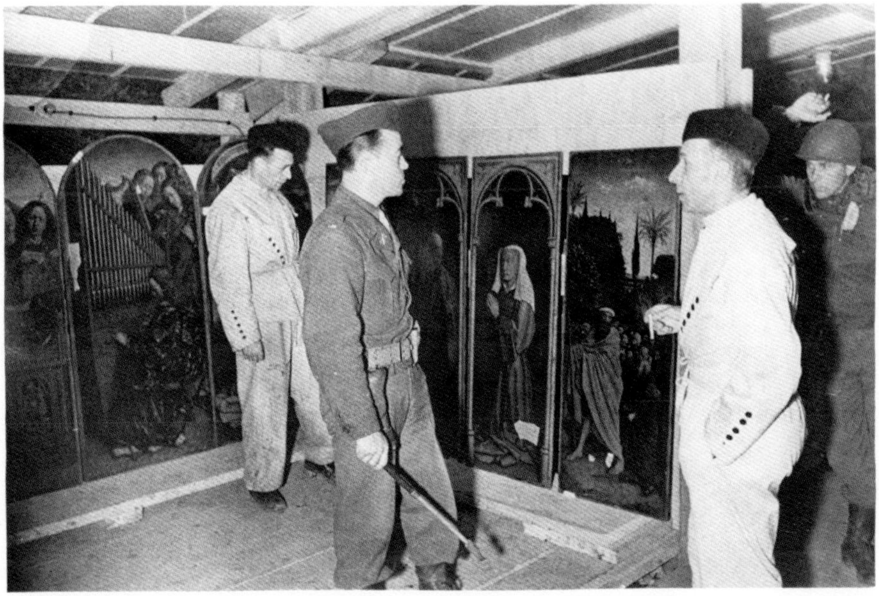

The Allies found the looted 'Lamb of God' altarpiece at the end of the Second World War.

painting to Germany anyway. In 1944, it was hidden in a salt mine at Alt Aussee in Austria, together with 7000 other works of art. When Germany's last hopes of victory were dashed by the failure of the Ardennes Offensive, the officer in charge wanted to blow up the entire art collection at Alt Aussee, to stop it falling into the hands of 'World Jewry'. Thankfully, others, who informed the Allies of the presence of the works of art, frustrated his insane plan. The painting was narrowly saved from destruction on 8 May 1945. It was exhibited in Brussels for a while and given a thorough examination, before being returned to Ghent. The altarpiece then hung in its original place in the Vyd Chapel until 1986, when it was transferred for security reasons to a glass case in the former baptismal chapel of the cathedral (the 'De Villa Chapel').

THE RESTORATION OF THE ALTARPIECE (2012-17)

Although the altarpiece looks good for its advanced age, it has been clearly marked by the passage of time. Virtually no centuries-old monuments or works of art in our region have come down to us entirely intact: they have all had to be maintained and repaired over the years, often repeatedly. Ghent's great masterpiece is no exception. In our brief history of the painting, we mentioned that several restorations were carried out between the sixteenth and nineteenth centuries. It was on one such occasion that the painted predella from the bottom of the altarpiece was sadly lost. The Lamb of God was also cleaned and conserved during the twentieth century, including after its return from the Austrian saltmine in which it spent the Second World War.

The altarpiece underwent further conservation in 2010, accompanied this time by a thorough scientific examination sponsored by the Getty Foundation and conducted by a team of international experts. This revealed that the altarpiece was seriously damaged in many places, not least because of the various layers of varnish that now cover the original paint layer. Some of the earlier retouching and overpainting was likewise found to have done more harm than good. The 2010 study revealed, in short, that fundamental restoration of the masterpiece as a whole was highly desirable.

The first panels were removed for restoration in September 2012. Once again, a top international team was appointed to oversee this huge and delicate task, carried out by the specialist technicians of the Royal Institute for Cultural Heritage (KIK-IRPA) in Brussels. Ghent University is also taking this opportunity to perform further fundamental scientific research. The restoration work itself is being done at a specially equipped unit at the Museum of Fine Arts (MSK) in Ghent, where visitors can observe it at any time. Throughout this period, the Caermersklooster provincial cultural centre is holding a permanent public exhibition on the Lamb of God, accompanied by a series of temporary displays. If all goes to plan, the whole of the altarpiece should be back, complete, in its familiar surroundings at St Bavo's Cathedral by the end of 2017. It will continue to move and amaze thousands of visitors, just as it did in the past, but now with its fresh, youthful glory restored.

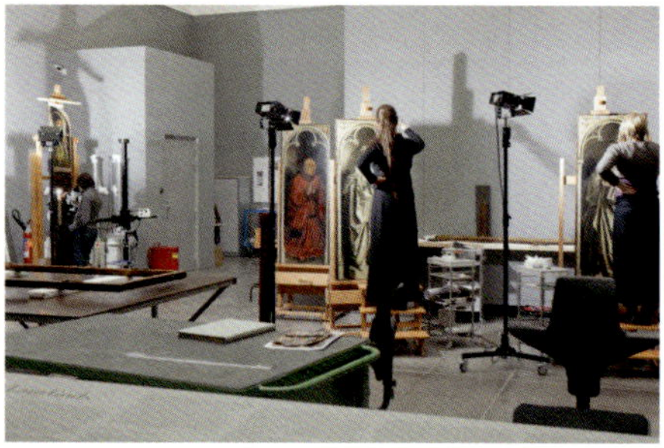

The restoration of the altarpiece is being done at a specially equipped unit at the Museum of Fine Arts in Ghent.

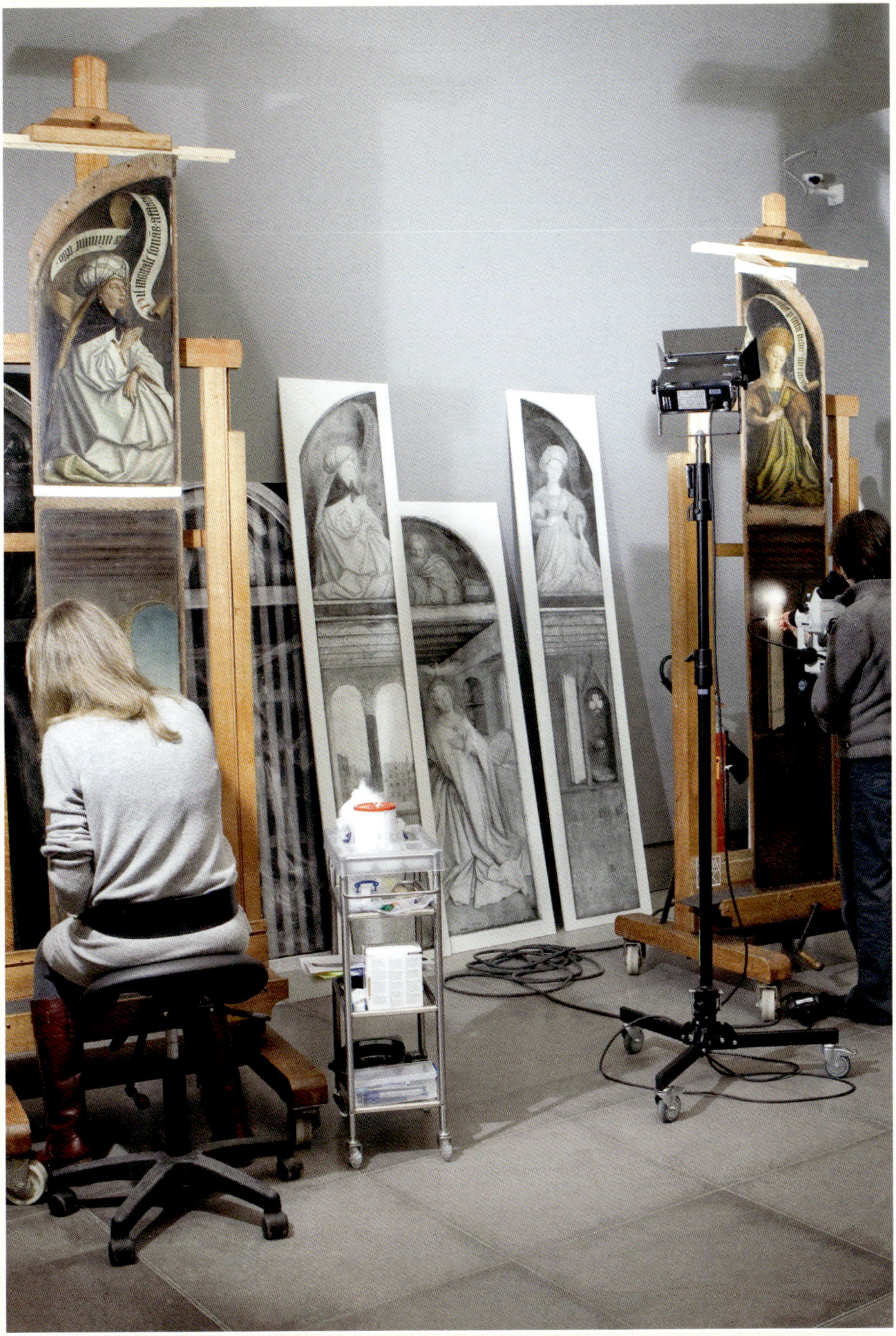

– 5 –

DESCRIPTION OF THE GHENT ALTARPIECE

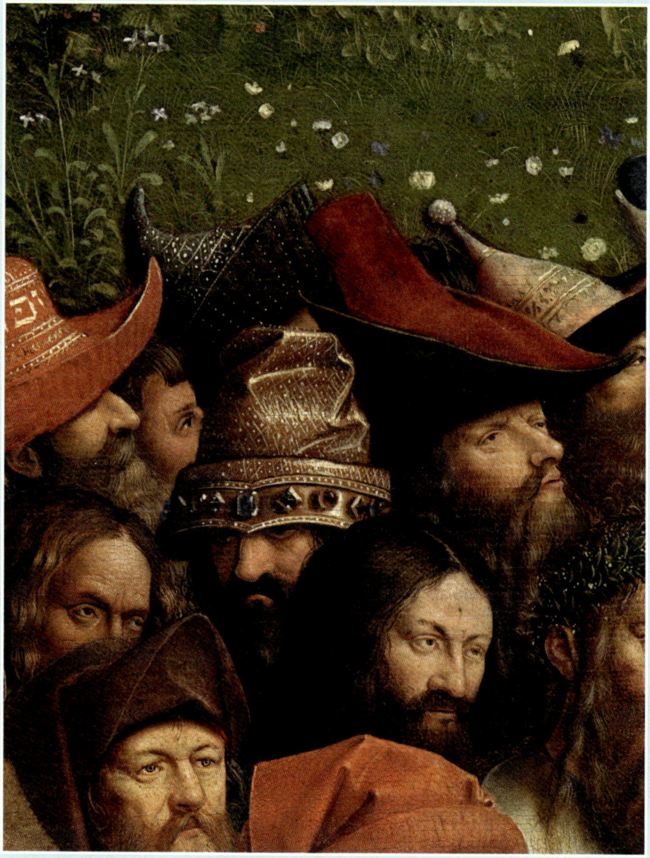

Medieval altarpieces often consisted of several panels. The best-known type is the triptych, in which the main religious theme is often shown in the centre panel, with the donors appearing in the side panels or wings. The donors may or may not be integrated in the presentation of the centre panel. Triptychs that were to be shown both open and closed had linked religious scenes painted on the reverse of the wings, and it was these that churchgoers would see whenever the altarpiece was closed. Depending on their size, the wings could be made up of various different panels. The Adoration of the Lamb is constructed in the form of a triptych, comprising a total of 24 panels. The altarpiece includes four images linked to the circumstances and location in which it was painted: the donors – Jodocus Vyd and his wife Elizabeth Borluut, and the two biblical St Johns. John the Baptist is included as the saint to whom the church was dedicated, while St John the Evangelist was the author of the Book of Revelation, from which the central scene is taken. The religious theme is spread across the remaining twenty panels. At first sight, the various scenes appear fairly disparate – Adam and Eve, figures from Heaven, a crowd surrounding the Lamb, the Annunciation of Christ's birth, prophets and sibyls. The scale of the figures – especially those on the insides of the wings – also varies sharply, creating a kind of iconographical split between the upper and lower registers. This has prompted a great deal of debate regarding the original thematic unity of the altarpiece. The overall composition is, in fact, entirely unique. What is more, X-rays have shown that the iconographical programme was adjusted several times during the execution of the painting.

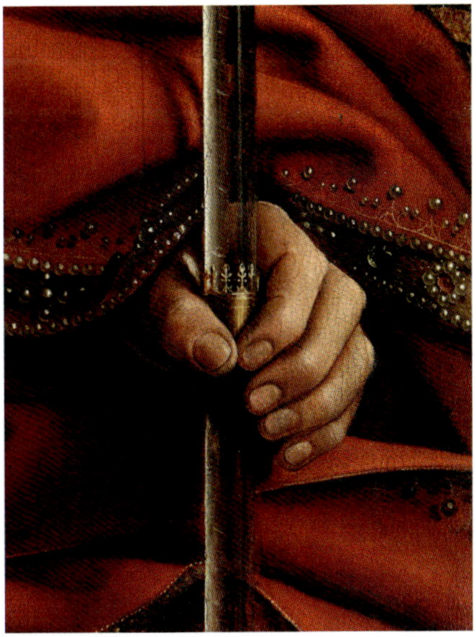

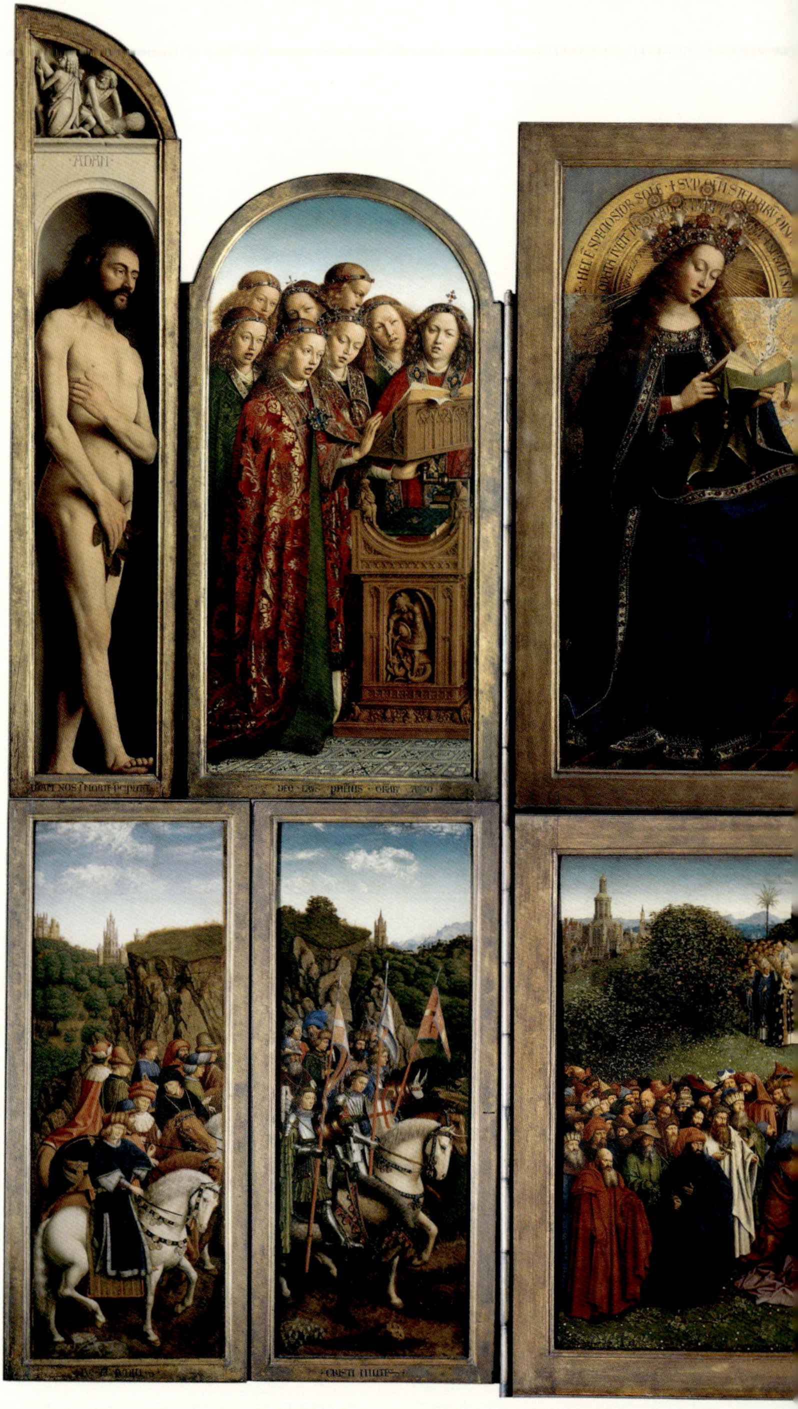
ADAM

THE OPEN ALTARPIECE

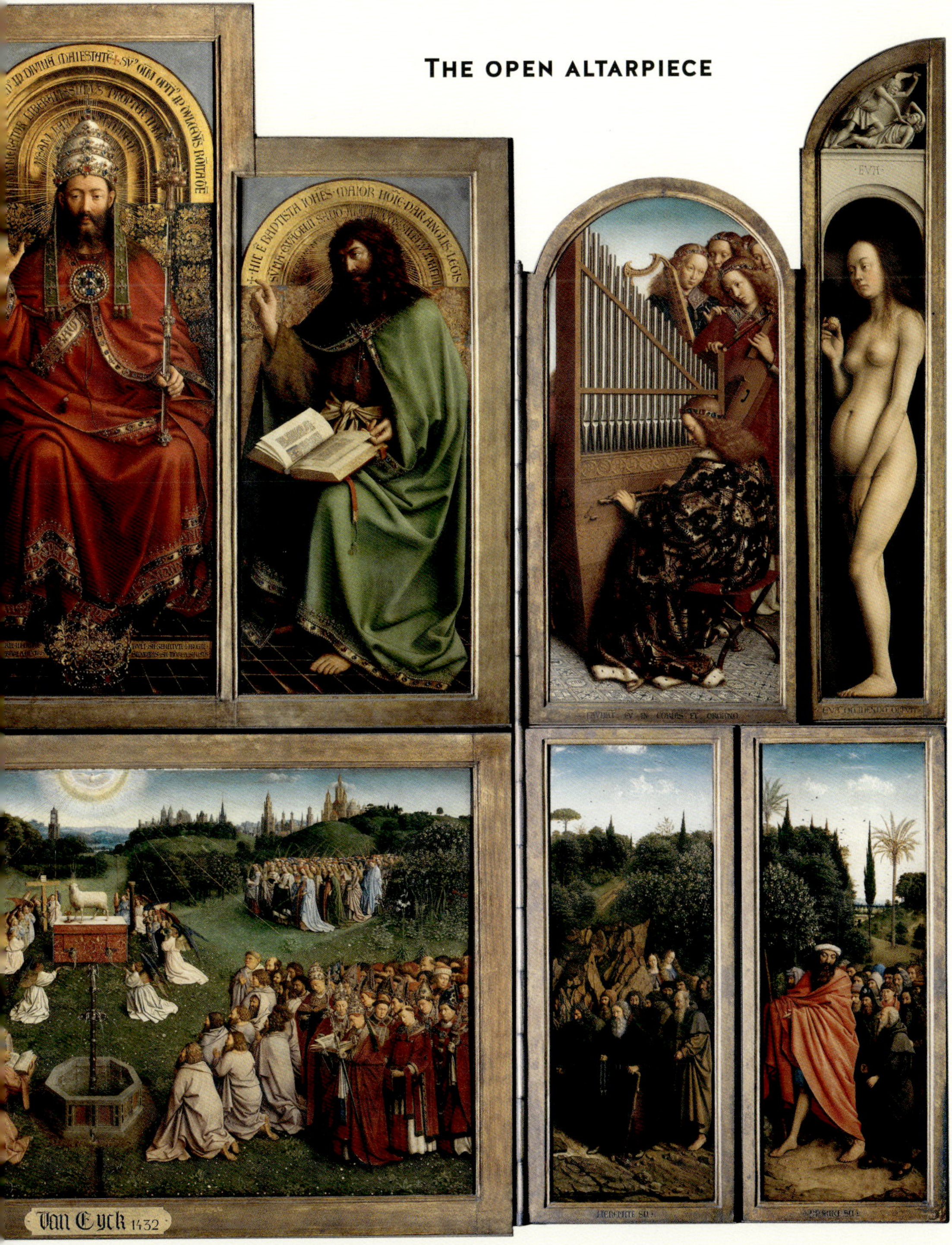

The Virgin Mary
Christ (or God the Father)
St John the Baptist

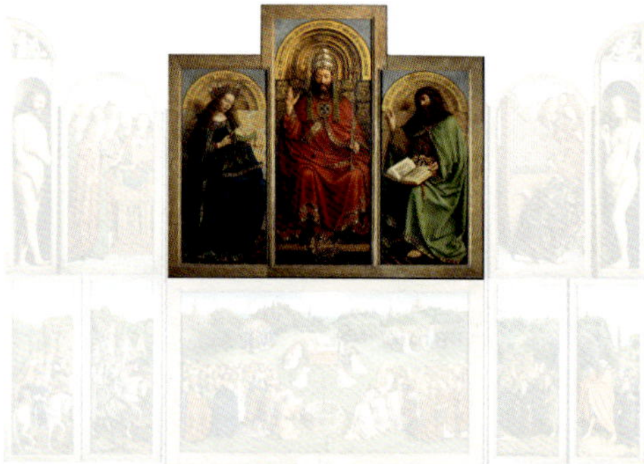

These panels immediately catch the eye of everybody who enters the chapel. Three seated figures – blue, red and green; God, flanked by the Virgin Mary and St John the Baptist – fill the centre of the upper register. There is persuasive evidence that Hubert van Eyck was responsible for these marvellous figures. The way he draped their robes lends them a monumentality hitherto not seen in Flemish painting.

The motif of these three figures alongside one another is extremely traditional. It arose in Byzantine art as a representation of the Deësis – the Greek word for 'supplication'. The image appears to be rooted in the Last Judgement, in which Christ is shown as judge, enthroned in the centre, with his mother Mary and his forerunner, John, kneeling in prayer, as intercessors. Images of the Deësis also appeared frequently in other contexts. It is this frequency, indeed, that makes it so difficult to identify the central figure in the painting.

This figure has been widely identified as God the Father, overseeing the story of the Salvation. He wears a papal tiara – an attribute normally associated with the Father – there are no wounds in his hands, and he is wearing shoes. All of this suggests God the Father, rather than Christ, who is usually, though not invariably,

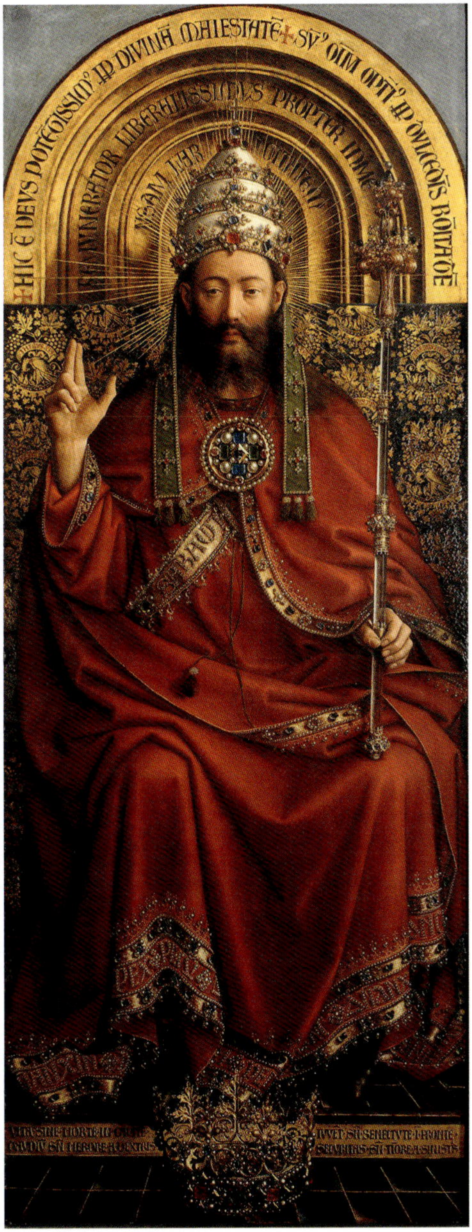

shown with the wounds in his hands and feet. He holds a sceptre, whereas Christ is more commonly portrayed with a book. The words on the back of the throne – 'This is the Almighty God through His Divine Majesty' – would also appear to apply to God the Father. The text on the golden stole, meanwhile – (Dominus Deus) Sabaot (Lord of Hosts) – refers to the Father during the Sanctus of the Mass. The identification as God the Father would also match the Trinitarian reading of the altarpiece. Christians refer to God as the Trinity – Father, Son and Holy Spirit. The lower part of the centre panel shows the Son – Christ – in the shape of the Lamb, with the Holy Spirit – in the guise of a dove – hovering above him. According to this interpretation, God the Father at the top would complete the Trinity. All the same, there are persuasive arguments to the effect that the figure is, in fact, that of Christ. The tapestry adorning the back of the throne, for instance, features a repeating pattern comprising three clear references to Jesus. The first is the pelican, which pierces its chest to feed its young with its own

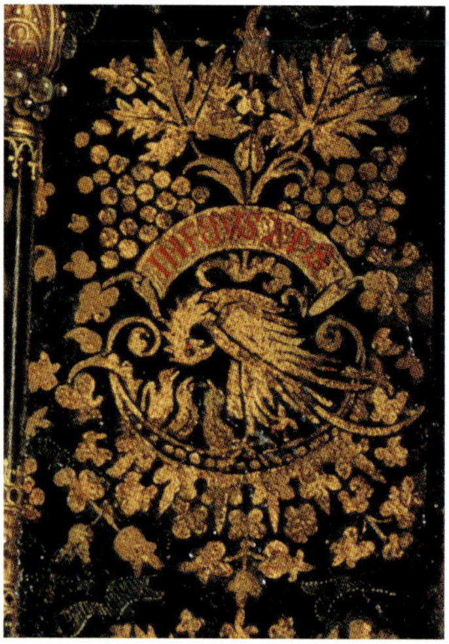

blood. This served for hundreds of years as an unambiguous symbol of the Eucharist, in which Christ offered his blood to the faithful. The vines are another clear reference to communion wine, while the banderole above the pelican contains the name 'Jesus Christ'. The Deësis motif, to which we referred a moment ago, is also very significant in this instance. In all Christian art, there is no known instance of an icon or painting in which God the Father is shown between the Virgin Mary and John the Baptist. It is Jesus who appears in that position without exception. If the figure in the Ghent Altarpiece is, indeed, meant to be the Father, then this is the only painting in which the trio of the Virgin, the Father and the Baptist appears together, and the only one in which John the Baptist points to the Father. Given the importance of traditional rules and ease of identification at the time, it thus seems highly unlikely that Van Eyck was referring here to God the Father. Churchgoers were well aware that John the Baptist always points out Christ. The fact that Jesus also appears in the altarpiece in the guise of the Lamb does not diminish this argument, as other figures – the Virgin, John the Baptist and the Holy Spirit – also appear more than once. What is more, we know of many paintings and sculptures containing both the enthroned Christ and a lamb. The issue will, nevertheless, have to remain open. Some scholars believe that Van Eyck deliberately blended aspects of the Father and the Son. Another possible explanation is that Van Eyck wanted to present the figure of 'God' in his Trinitarian unity – as Father, Son and Holy Spirit all at once.

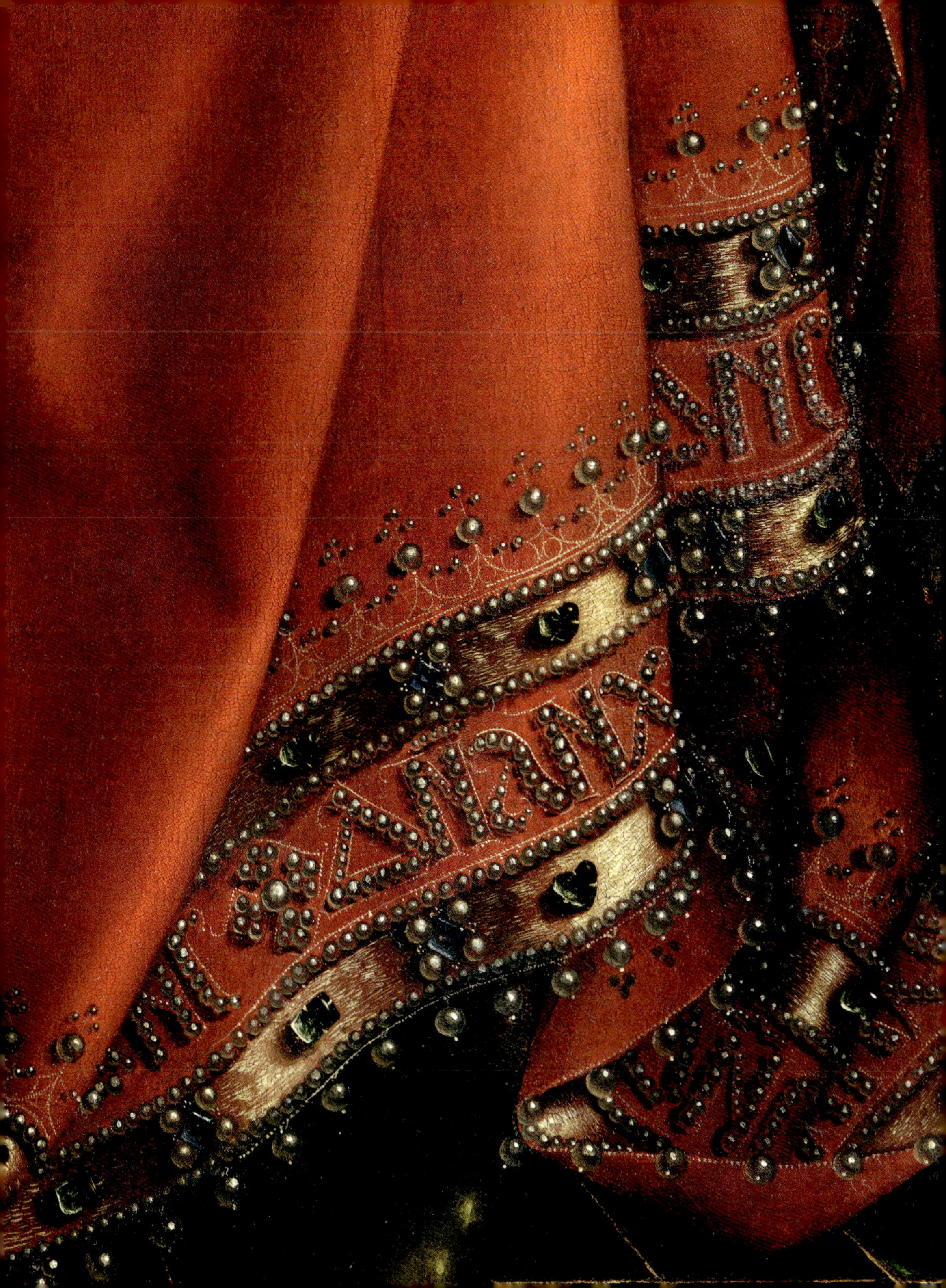

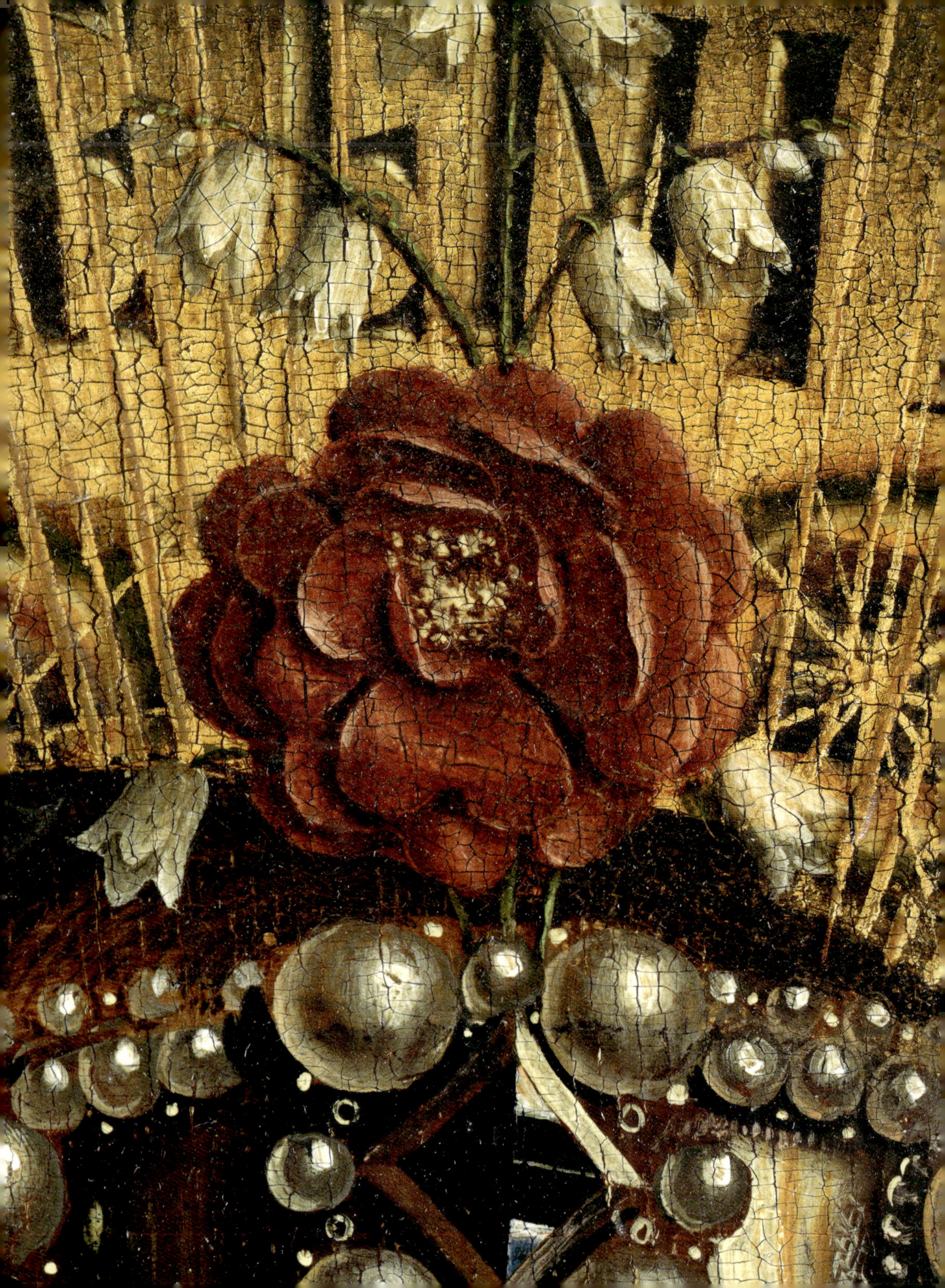

A modest, young Madonna – the Mother of God – sits at the right hand of this mysterious figure (the viewer's left). Her serene face looks out from beneath a cascade of hair. Dressed in a deep-blue robe, the darkness of which is alleviated by a golden hem, decorated with jewels, she is absorbed in a prayerbook. Twelve stars surround her fabulous crown – an allusion to the Book of Revelation. The crown itself incorporates four types of flower, all of which were Marian symbols: lilies (virginity, purity), roses (love, suffering, purity), columbines (humility) and lily-of-the-valley (linking the Song of Songs, 2:1, to the Virgin Mary).

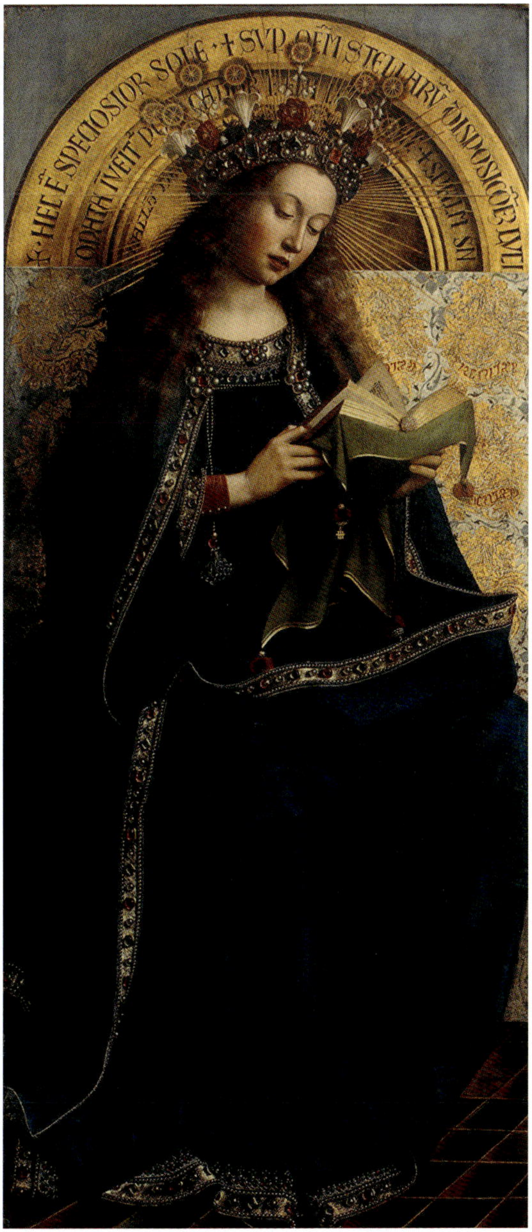

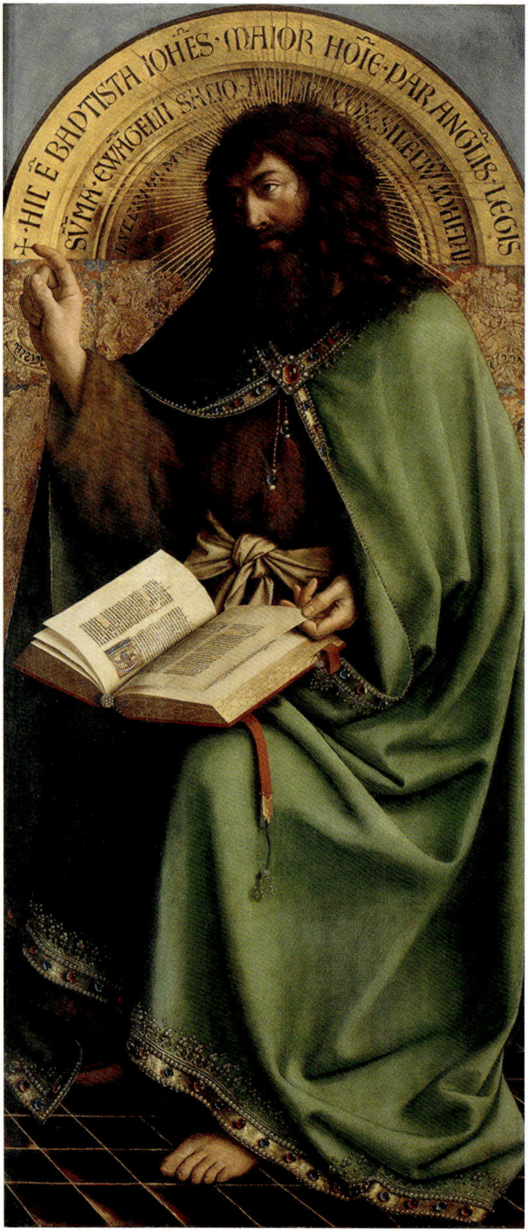

The figure on the other side is John the Baptist, whom Christians believe to have been the last Old Testament prophet. A stately green cloak covers his original costume – the ascetic camel-hair tunic that he wore when preaching the doctrine of baptism on the banks of the Jordan. As was customary in medieval images, he points to the Messiah with his right index finger. In the book that rests on his knees, we make out the word Consolamini (Take comfort), which begins a prophecy in the Book of Isaiah that was interpreted in the Gospels as a reference to John the Baptist and which announces the coming of the Messiah.

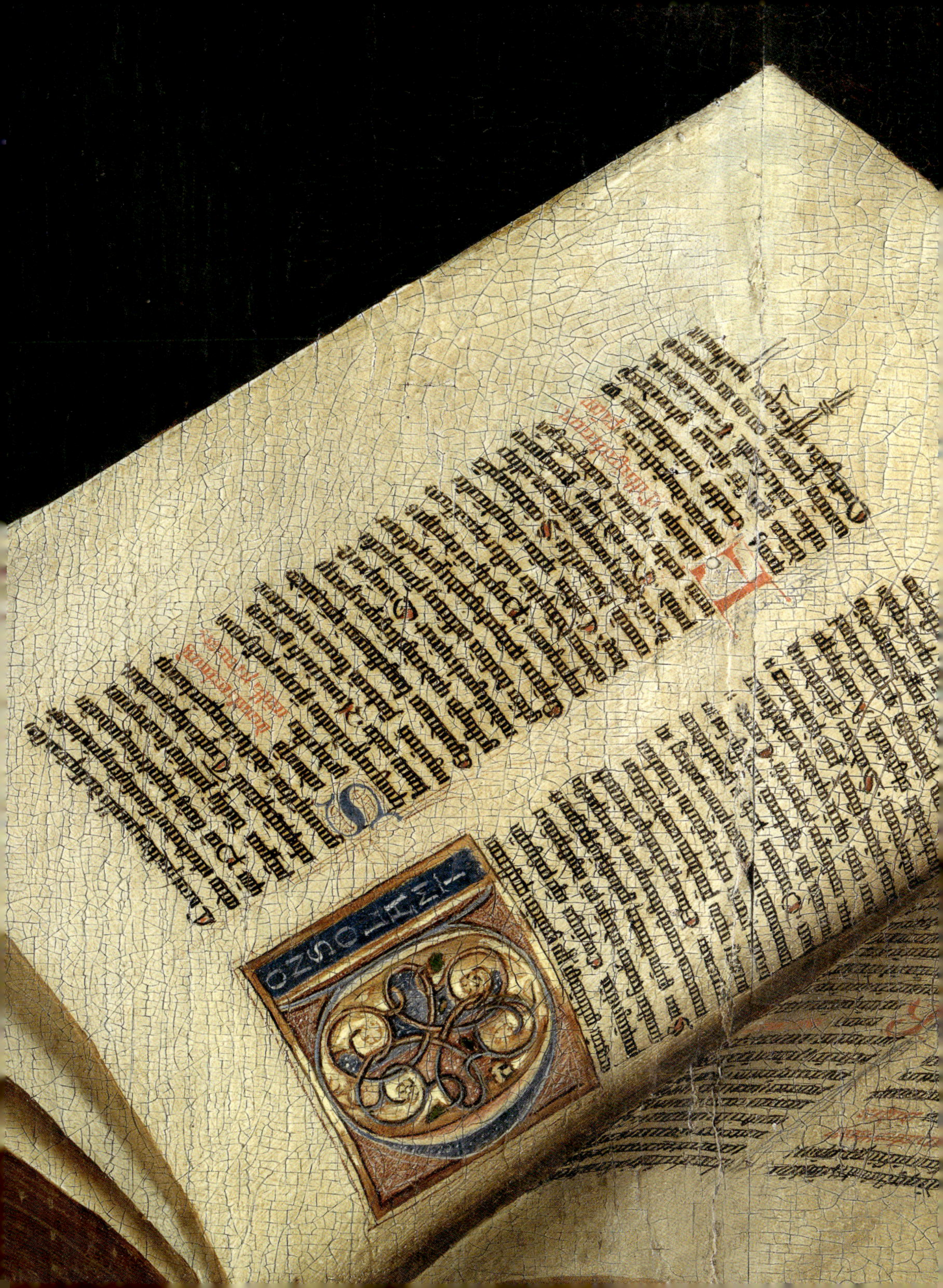

Angels singing
Angels playing music

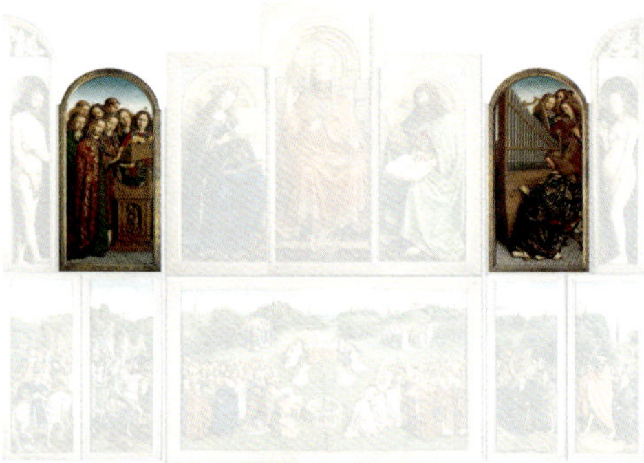

Hubert van Eyck painted groups of heavenly singers and musicians on either side of the three central figures. Although they do not have wings, they are invariably identified as angels. Eight of them, dressed in brocade copes, stand around a lectern singing the polyphonic music that flourished at the Burgundian court in Van Eyck's period. The angelic musicians on the other side do not wear copes, but tunics, possibly to leave their hands free. Alone among the musicians, the organist (possibly St Cecilia) wears an ermine-trimmed robe of dazzling splendour. Like God's sceptre, the organ pipes and the hundreds of jewels leave the viewer open-mouthed at the technical brilliance with which the artist(s) represented physical reality.

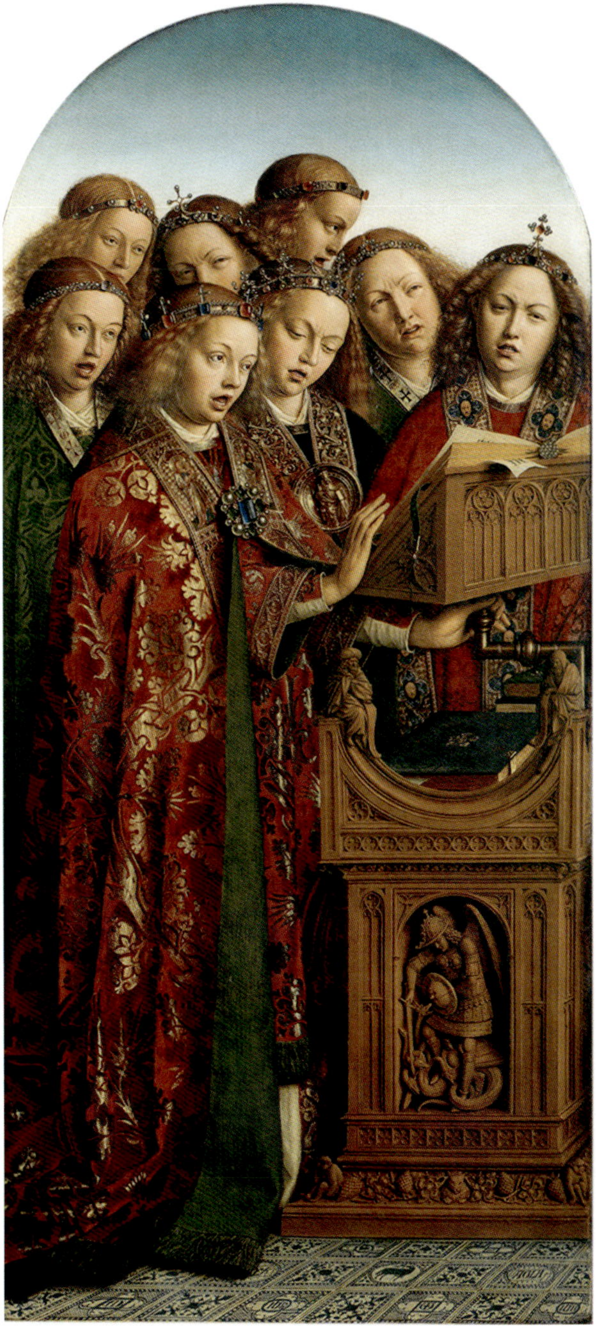

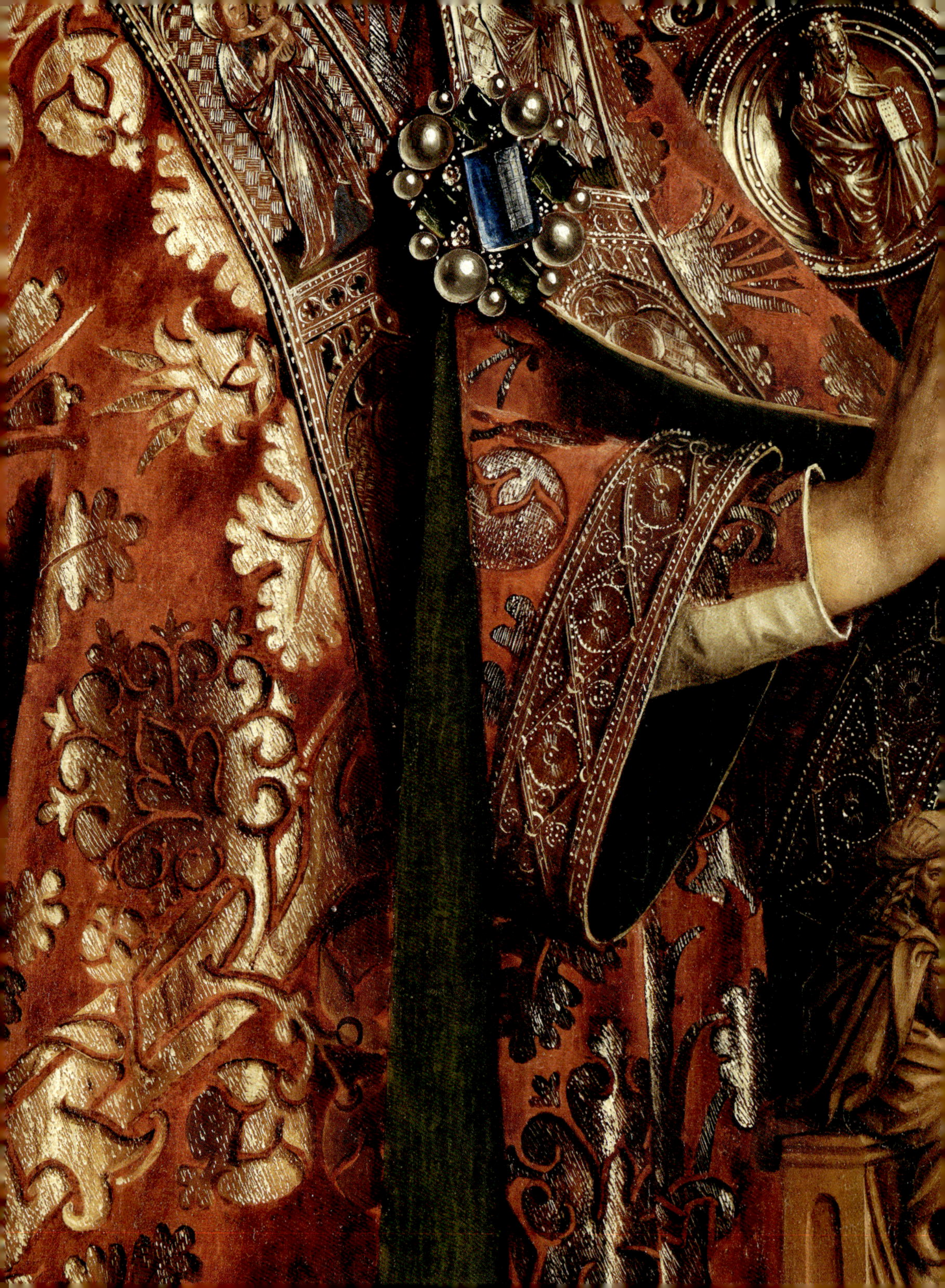

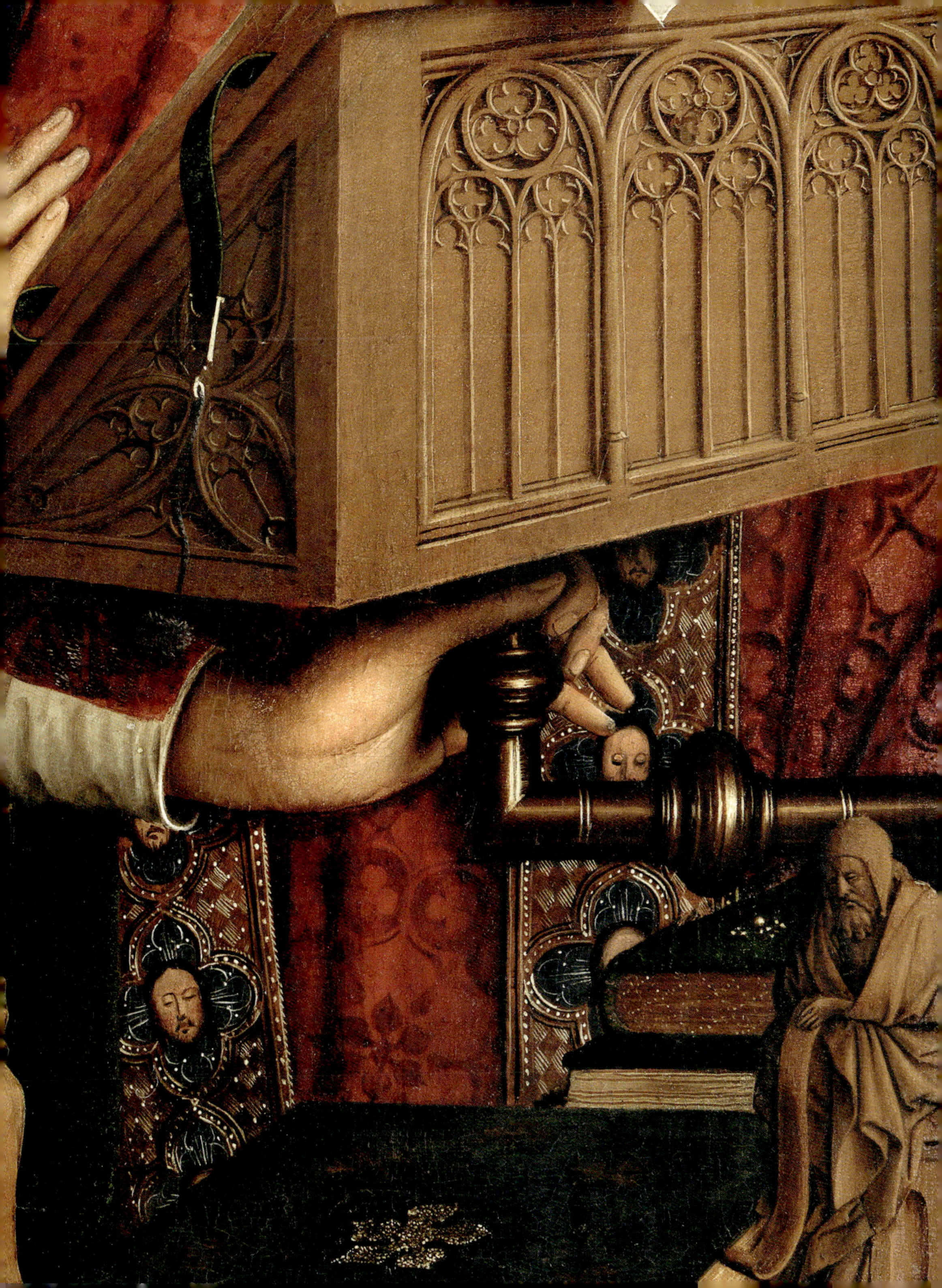

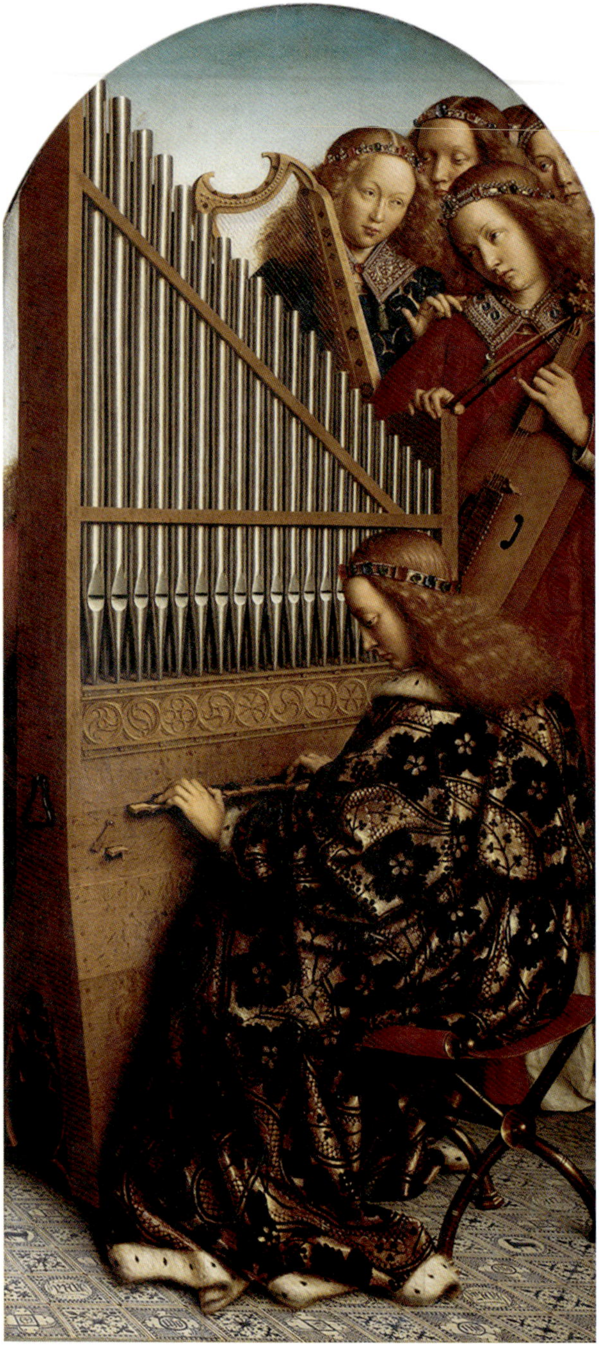

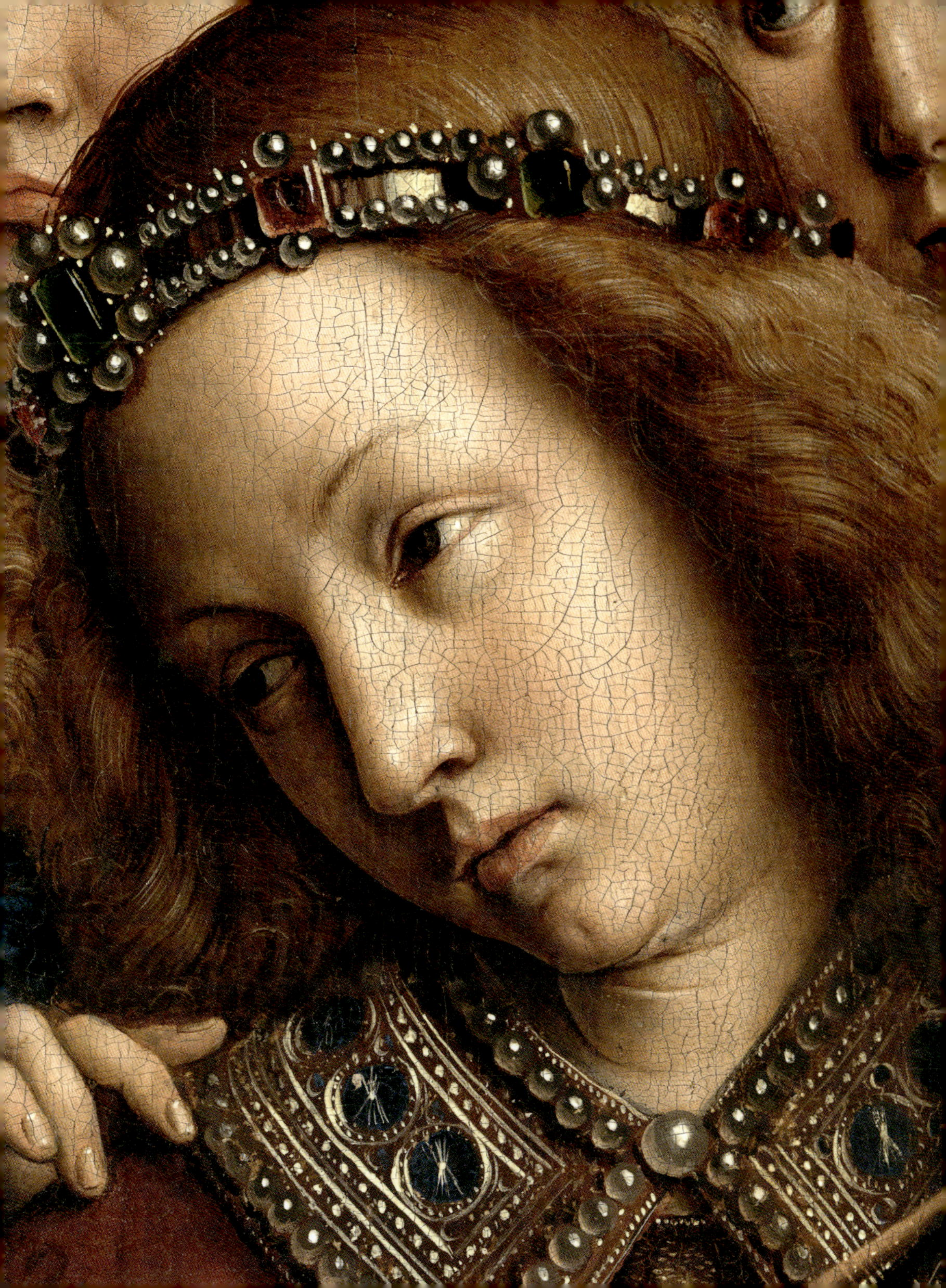

Adam
Eve

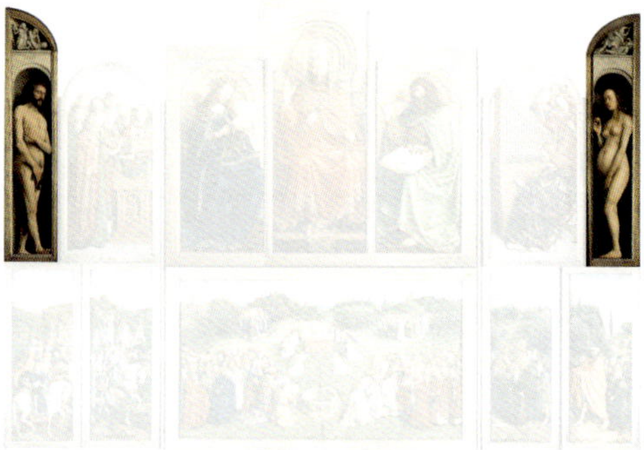

The biblical ancestors of all humanity occupy the outermost panels of the upper register. They stand in niches, which means that they are the only figures in the inside of the altarpiece who do not have the blue sky as their background. This serves to distinguish them from the heavenly figures. Yet, they are included in that company, because as the first sinners, they will also be the first to be saved. They symbolise the whole of humanity, which the Lamb will redeem from sin and death. Adam and Eve's serene gaze belies the texts, which state that through their sin, they brought death into the world. They are part of the static, undramatic atmosphere of the entire painting. Note the detail of Adam's foot, which extends beyond the edge of the frame, and Eve's fruit – not an apple, but a citrus fruit, which may be an allusion to the bitterness of the Fall.

Two pieces of imitation sandstone sculpture appear above Adam and Eve. These reliefs illustrate the first consequence of the couple's sin – Cain's murder of his younger brother, Abel. They serve as another symbol of the tragic history of humankind, which has suffered so much from fratricidal violence.

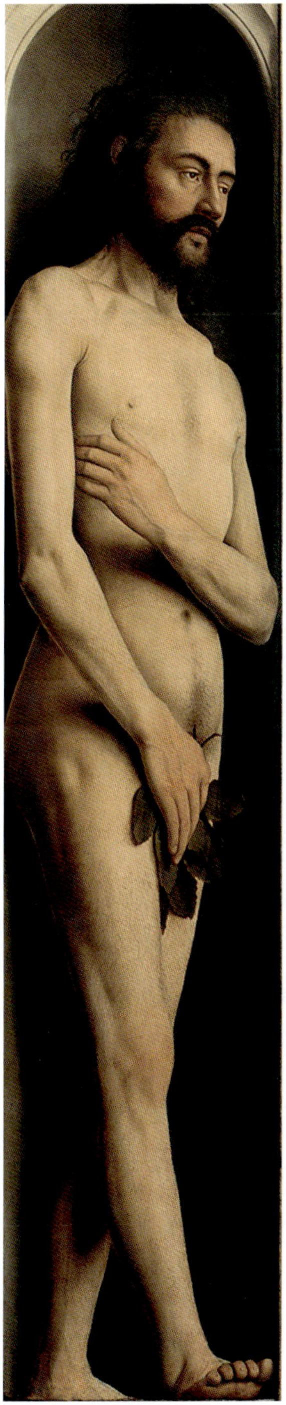

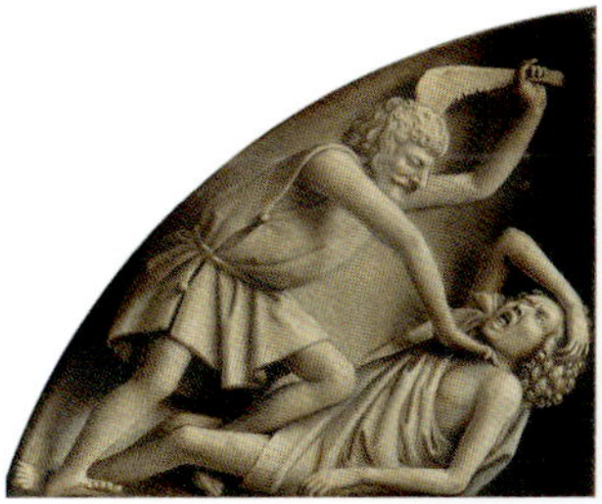

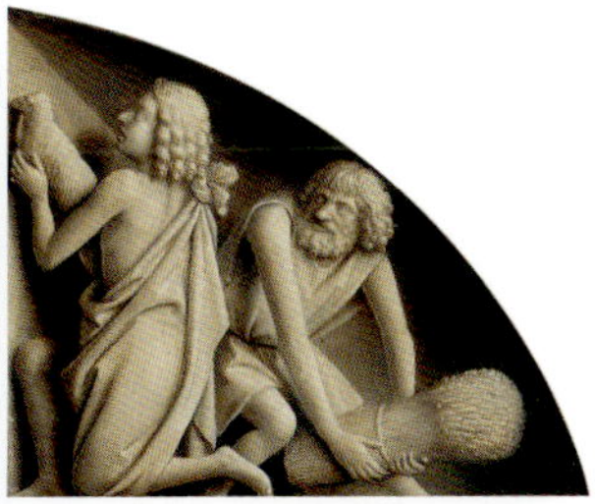

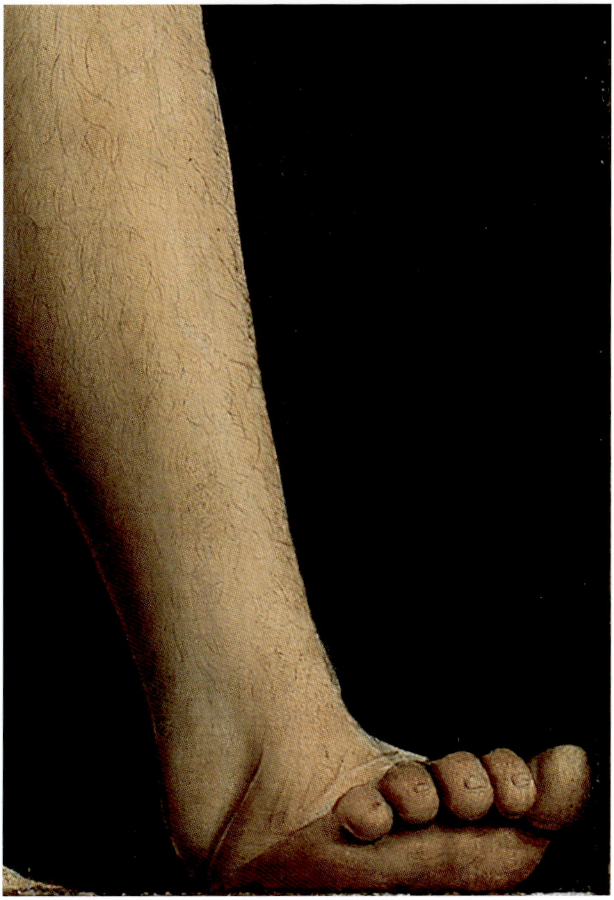

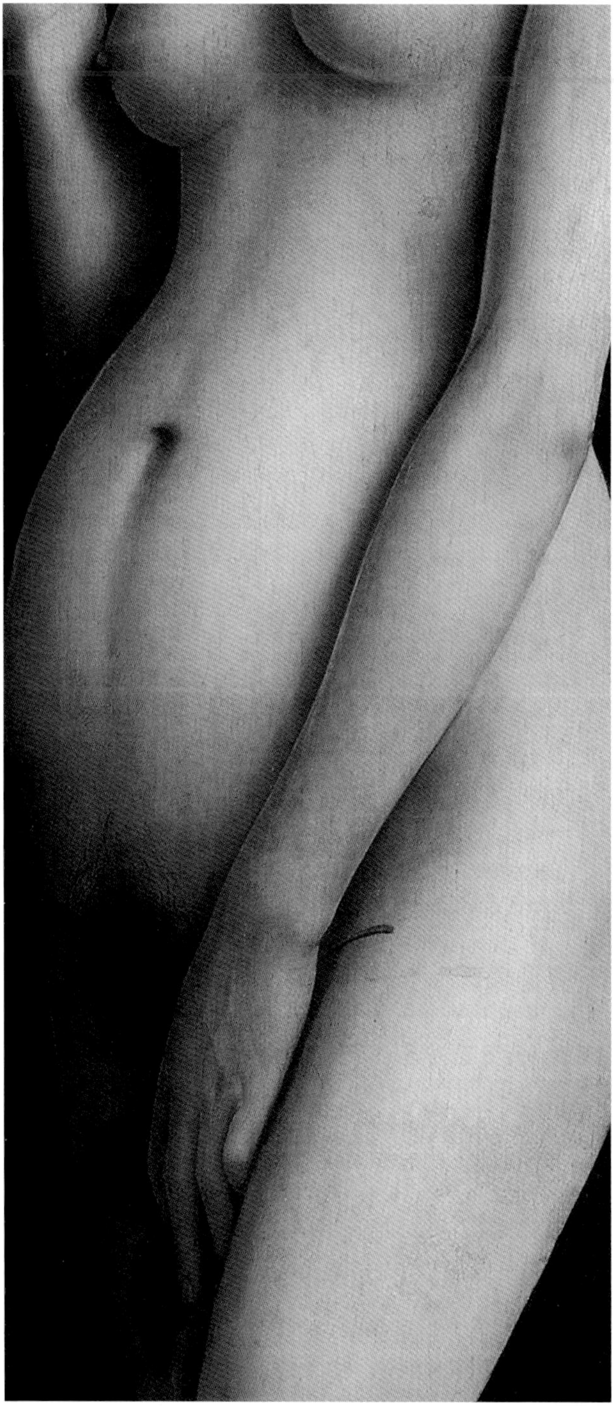

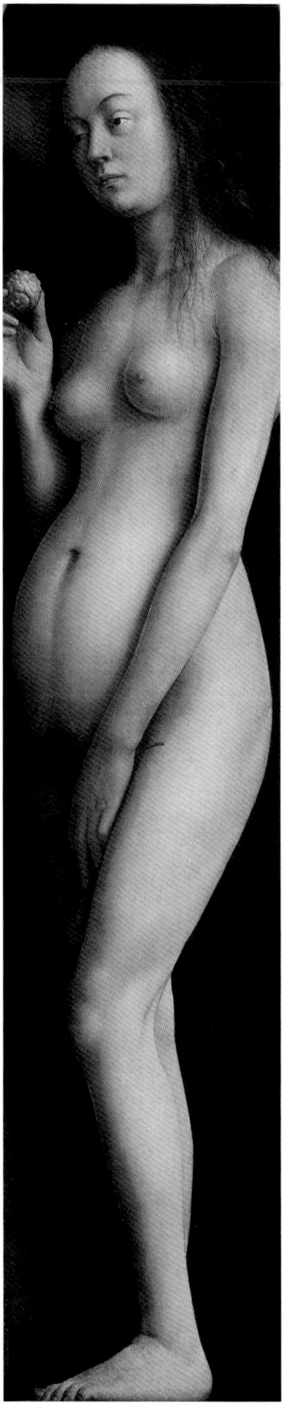

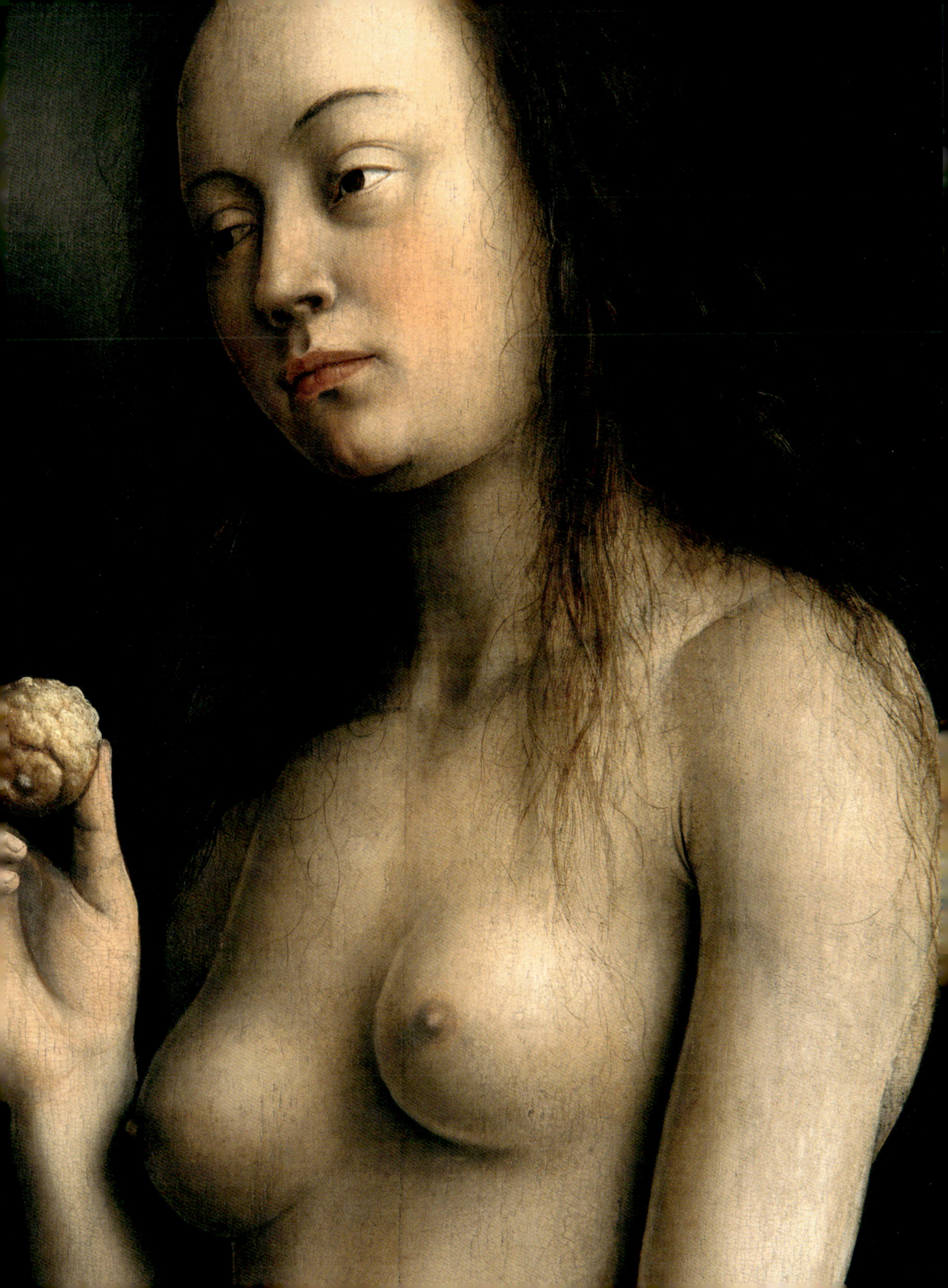

The Adoration of the Lamb of God

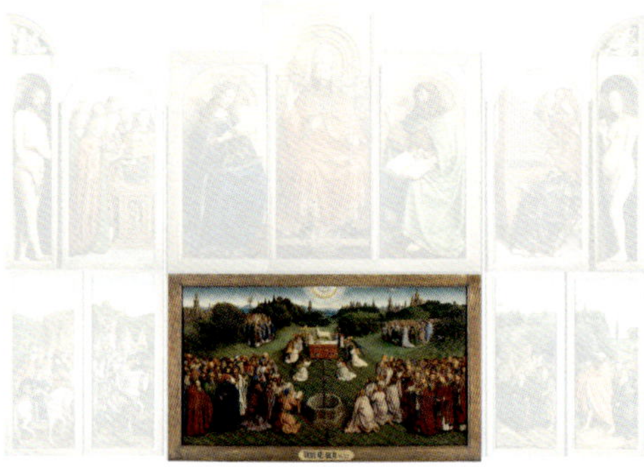

The viewer's full attention is drawn to the large centre panel, in which a divine liturgy is performed around the Lamb of God, Jesus Christ, in a green landscape with a high horizon. An altar stands in the middle on a small green mound, possibly representing Mount Zion. The Lamb stands erect on the altar – alive, but bleeding from a wound. Its blood spurts out into a chalice. The allusion is clear – Christ's death and resurrection – his sacrifice for humanity – are commemorated on the altar during every Mass. The scene as a whole refers to the Last Supper, when Jesus described the wine as his blood, which he was to shed for all humanity to earn the forgiveness of its sins.

Fourteen angels kneel in worship around the altar with the Lamb. The two in the foreground each wave a censer, while four in the background carry the instruments of Christ's Passion – the cross, the pillar of the Flagellation, the lance and the scourge with the sponge, the crown of thorns and the rods with which he was beaten.

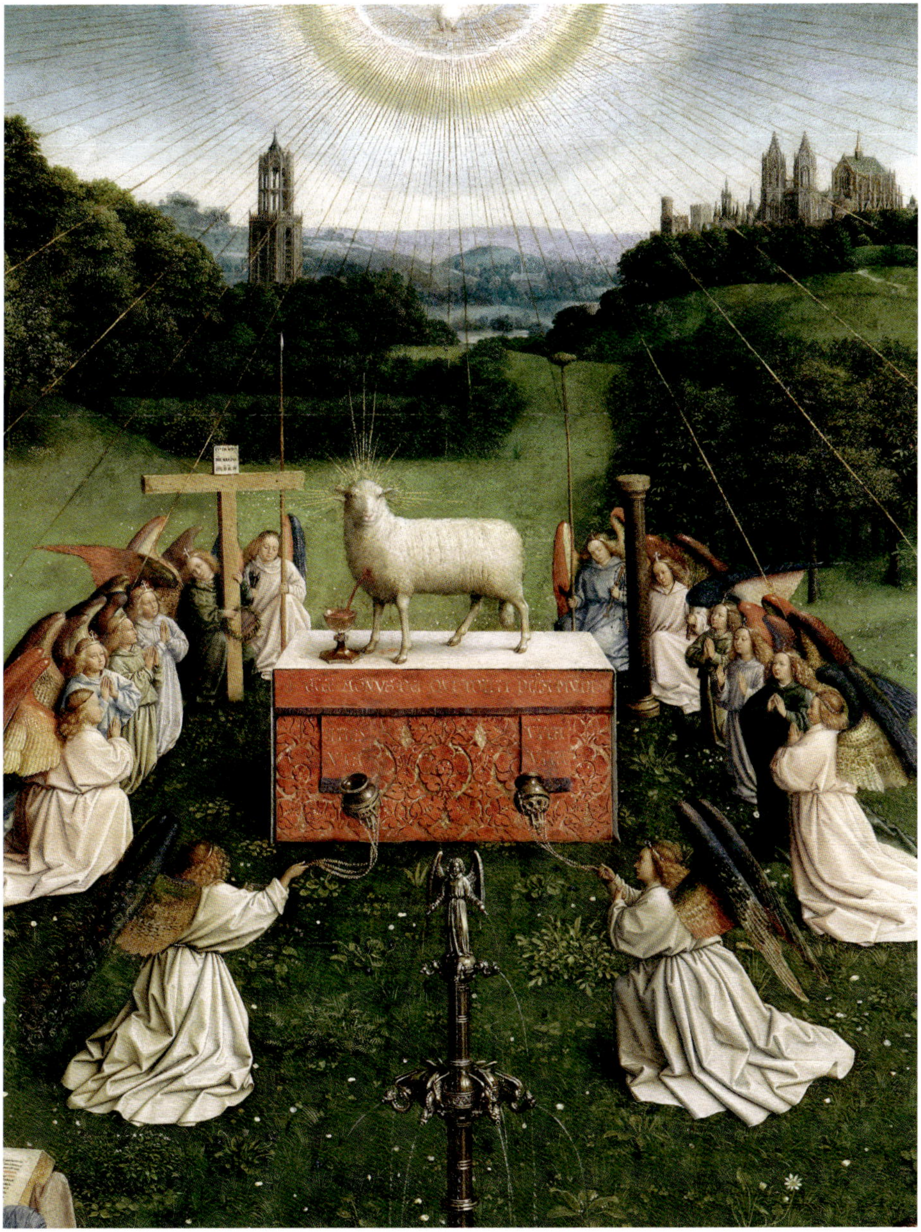

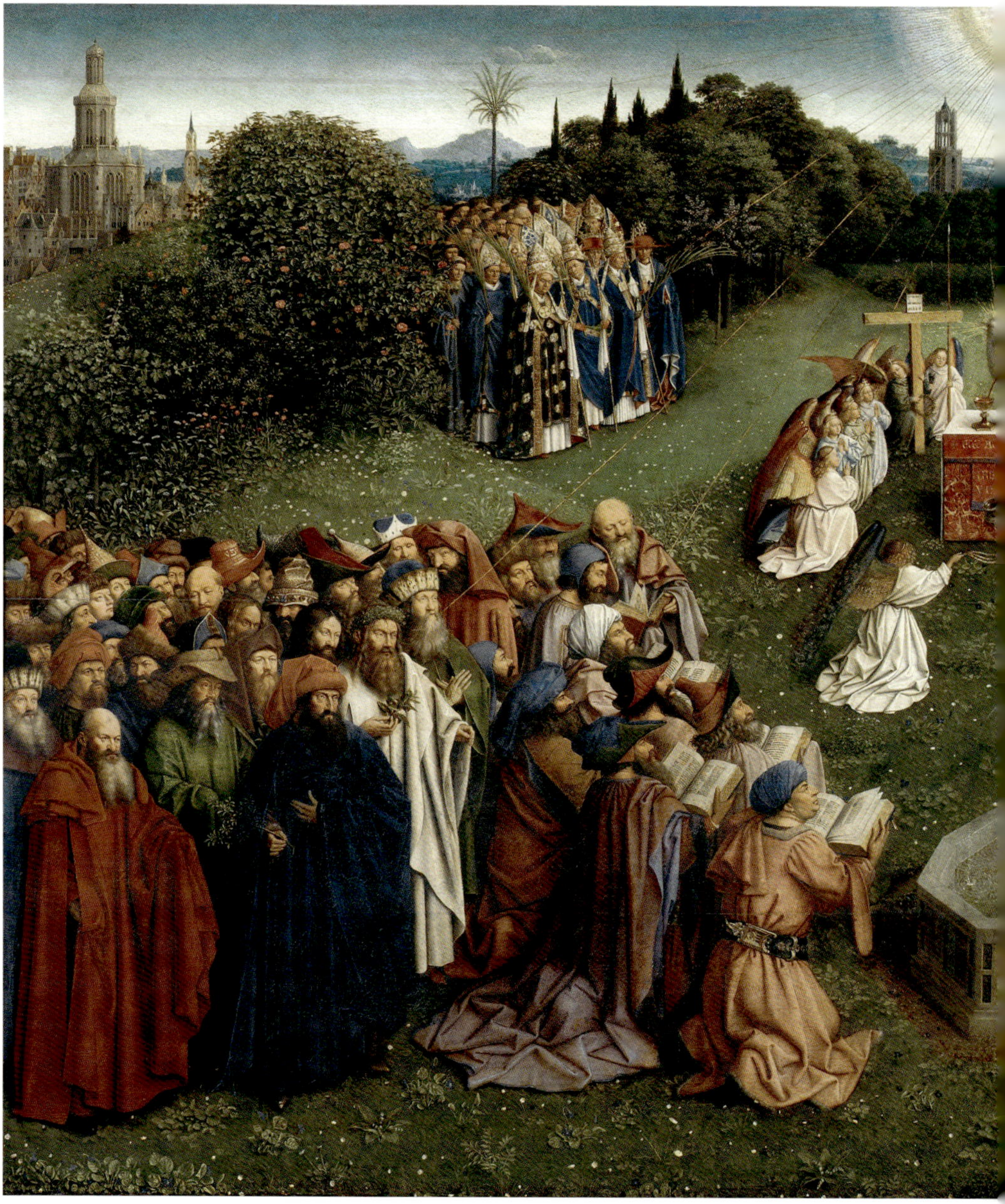

The difference in scale between the upper and lower parts of the altarpiece is very striking. The upper register is peopled with individual figures shown full size, in the

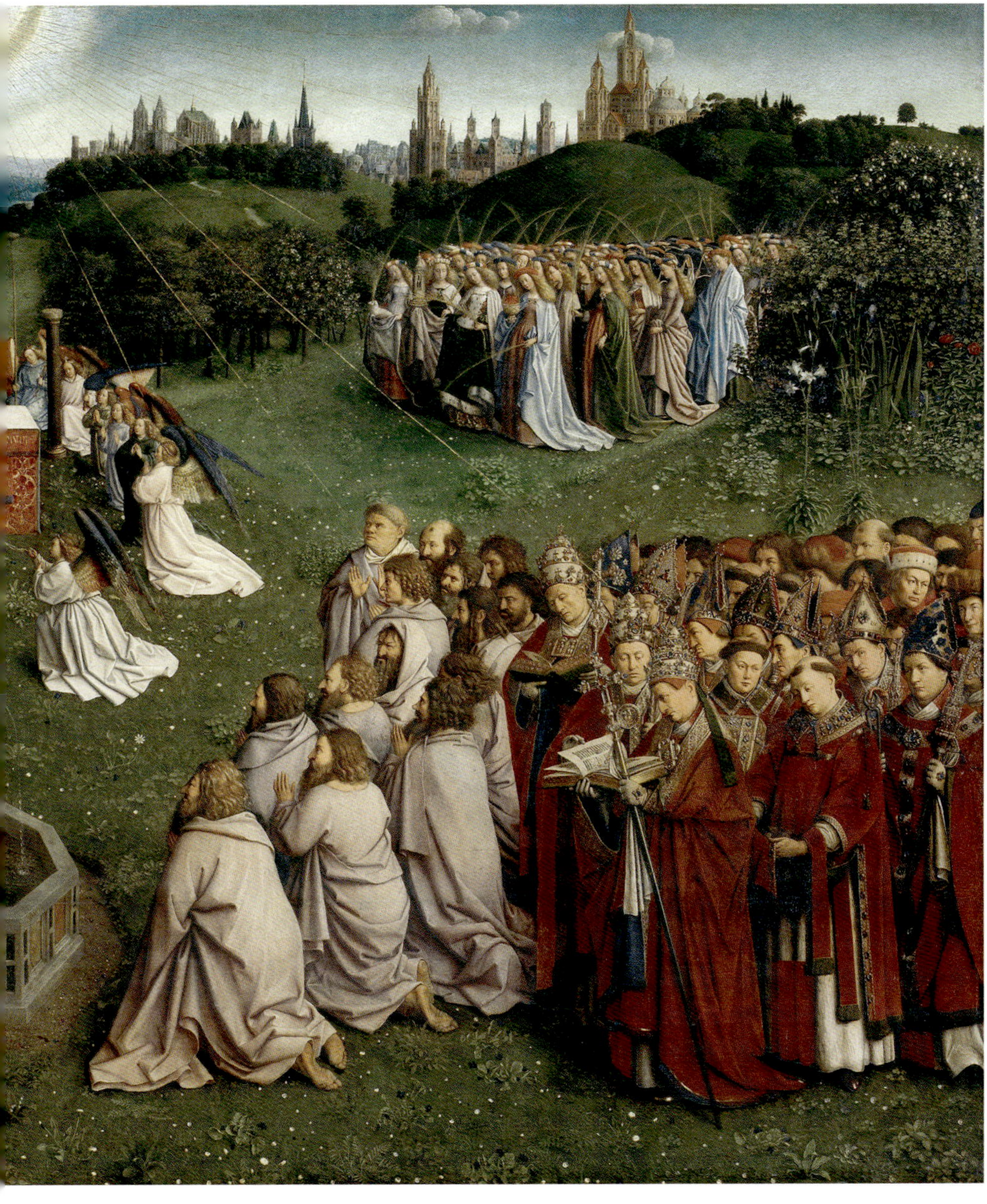

manner of Gothic altarpieces and icons. The lower one, by contrast, shows a landscape with large groups of people, presented on an entirely different scale.

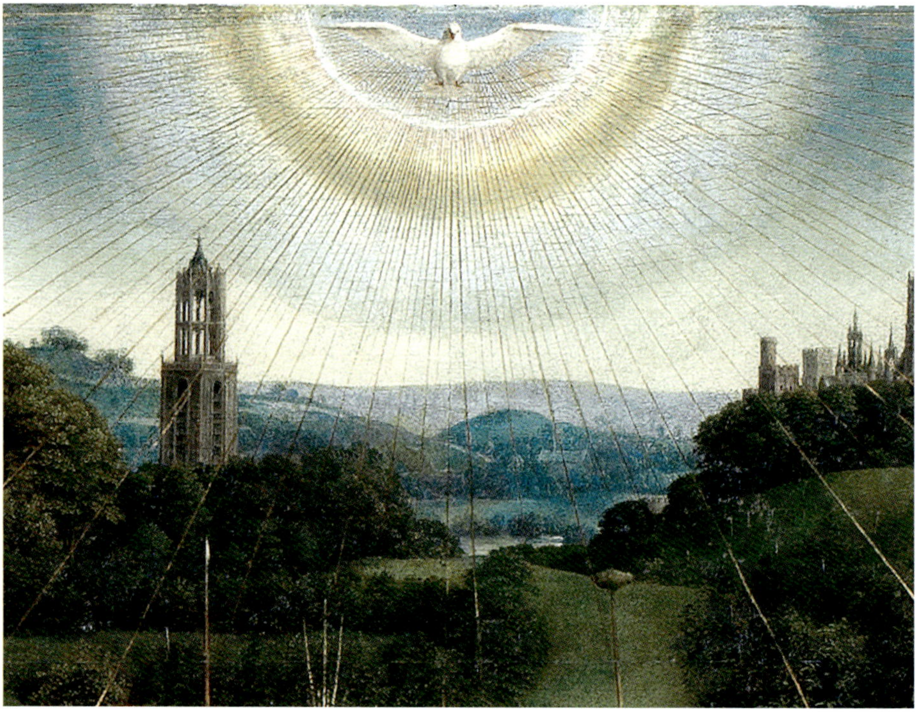

The Holy Spirit in the guise of a dove hovers above the scene, its triple aureole casting its rays across the entire panel. The action takes place within this divine light. Buildings can be seen all along the horizon, suggesting the new, heavenly Jerusalem from the Book of Revelation. Most of the buildings are imaginary, but one or two can be identified – the tower of Utrecht Cathedral, for instance, above and to the left of the lamb, and the dark tower of St Nicholas in Ghent, with its needle spire, on the

far right in the group of buildings between the Lamb and the holy women.

The central foreground contains a bronze fountain with an octagonal marble basin, from which twelve jets of water spray out. The number twelve represents the tribes of Israel and the Apostles, and is the perfect symbol for the Church as God's People. The basin is surrounded by a little moat, the bottom of which is sprinkled with precious stones. This, too, is an allusion to the description of the heavenly

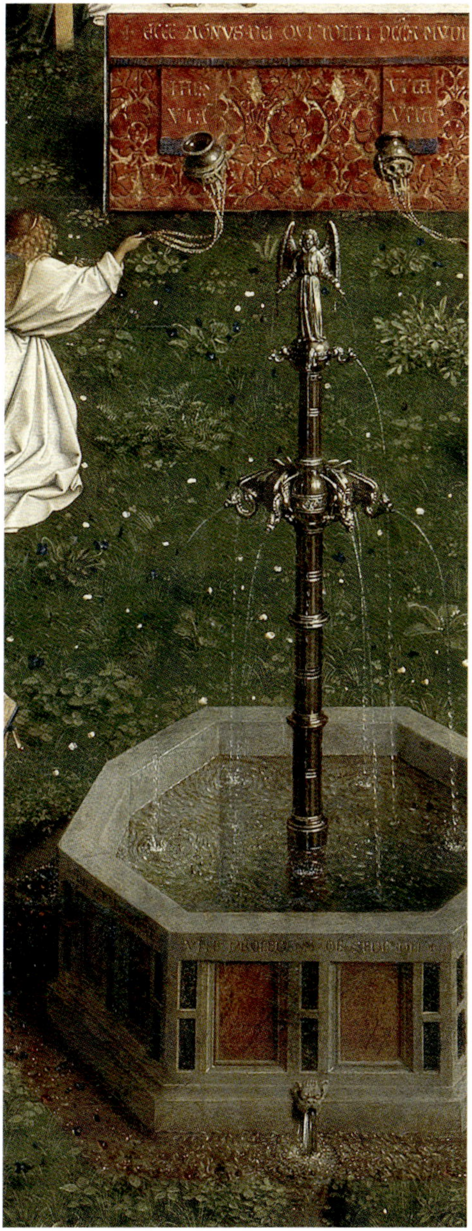

Jerusalem in the Book of Revelation, albeit with plenty of artistic licence. The lettering on the edge of the basin tells us that this fountain is the water of life that springs from the throne of the Lamb and has traditionally been viewed as a reference to the sacrament of Baptism. The octagonal fountain plays a key role in the composition of the altarpiece. Close inspection shows that the arrangement of the angels around the altar exactly corresponds to the octagonal shape of the fountain. The disposition of the prophets and apostles to the left and right of the fountain likewise follows its form. The entire central panel is thus composed around the triple repetition of the octagonal shape of the fountain. This is no coincidence. In the Middle Ages the number eight symbolised Easter, resurrection, salvation, new creation and eternal life – precisely what we find represented on the altarpiece. Moreover, the octagon was the preferred shape for baptisteries and fonts. The association of the water of life in the fountain with baptism is thus a natural one.

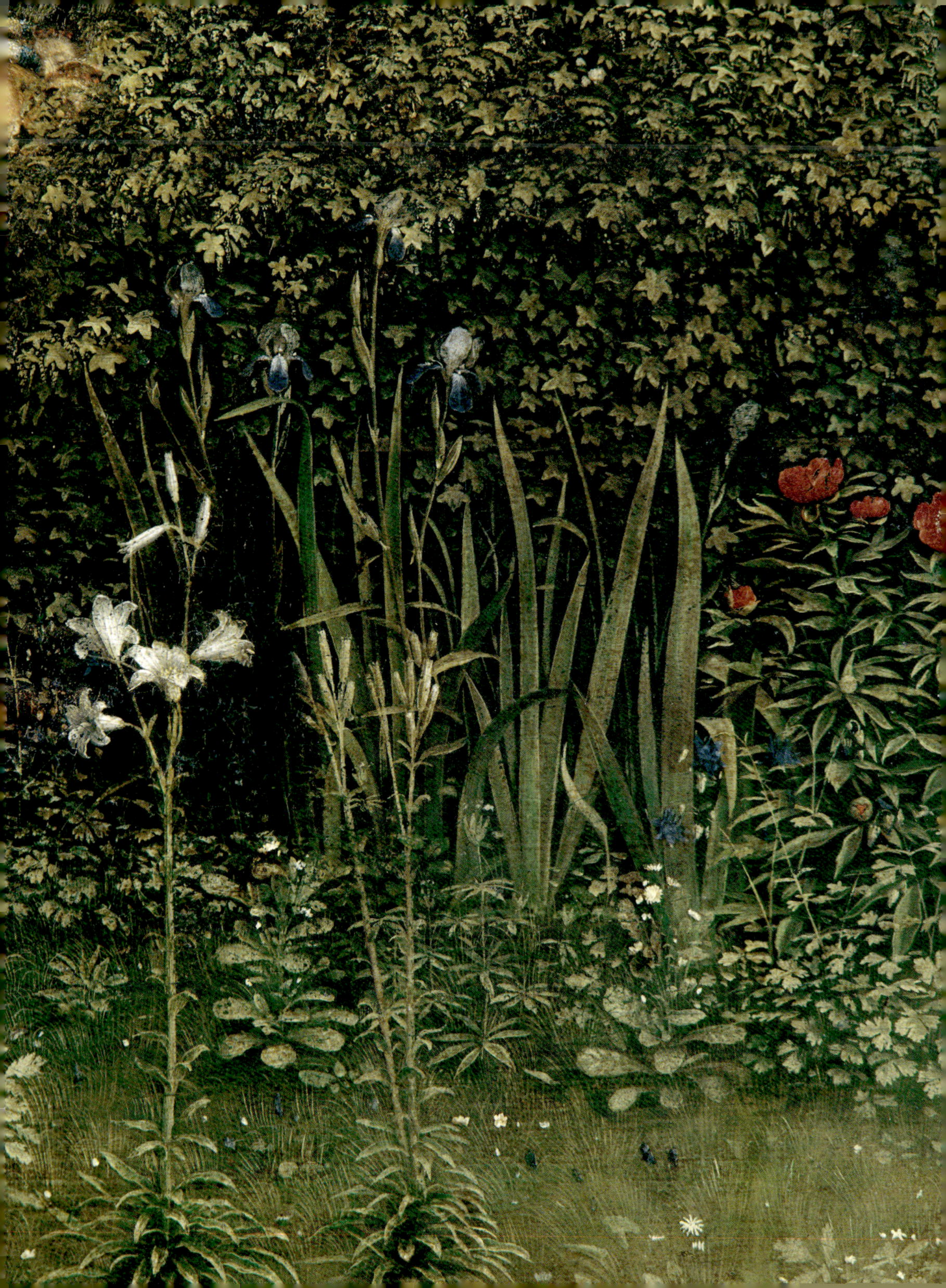

The landscape around the Lamb is covered with lush vegetation, which might be intended to suggest the Garden of Eden. Botanists have identified 42 different plant varieties in the painting, illustrating the artists' almost scientific interest in nature. The same admiring and analytical eye is evident here as in the representation of fabrics, precious stones, metals, wood and stone.

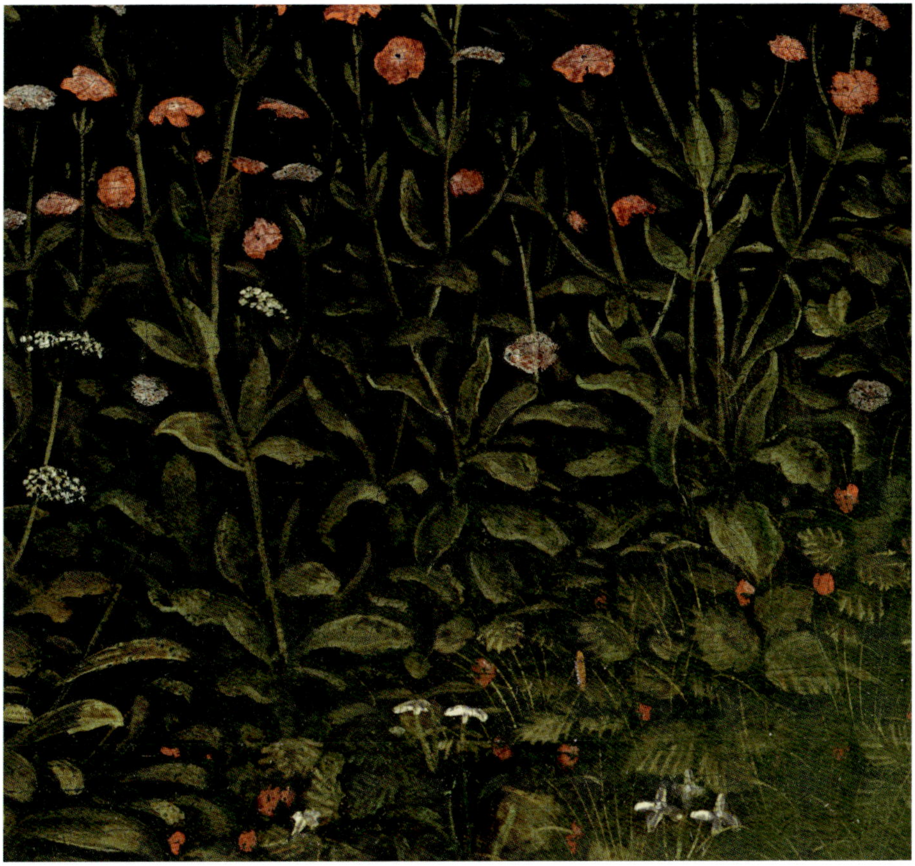

Groups of holy figures stream from between the trees into the meadow in which the liturgy is set.

In the left foreground we see twelve kneeling figures holding books. These are generally identified as the twelve 'Minor Prophets' from the Old Testament. The front row is then said to consist of the 'Major Prophets' (Isaiah, Jeremiah, Ezekiel and Daniel). Other suggestions include all manner of figures from the Old Testament and possibly also from the classical Antiquity. The figure in white with the laurel crown has been frequently identified as the Latin poet Virgil, who was highly esteemed in the Christian tradition. In the light of the hair style and the citrus fruit in his hand, however, it may well represent a Jewish figure. The group as a whole may refer to the 'great multitude that no one could count, from every nation, from all tribes and peoples and languages' referred to in Revelation (7:9), chosen to worship the Lamb. They included people who had not known of Christ or his Church, but who were saved none the less because of their unblemished lives.

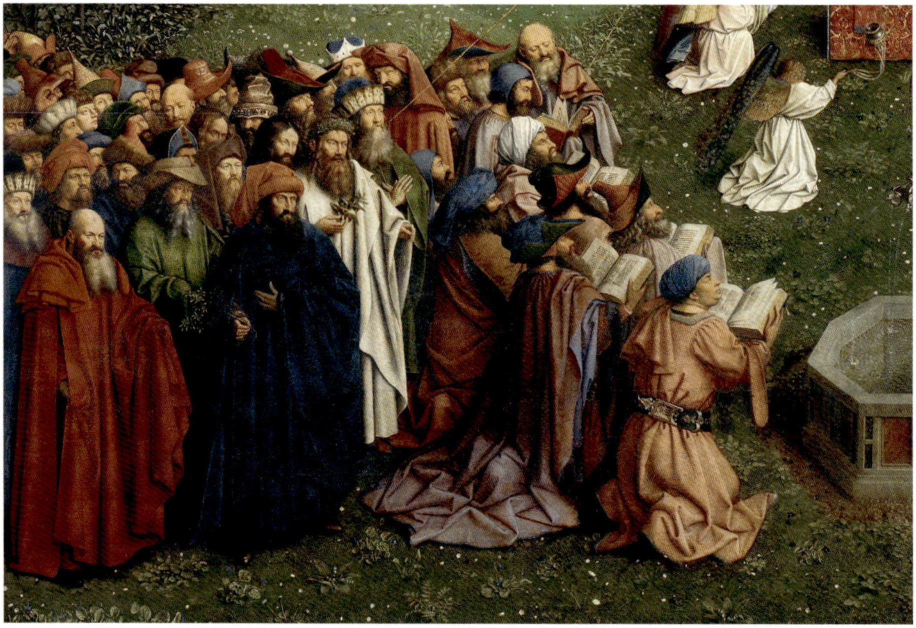

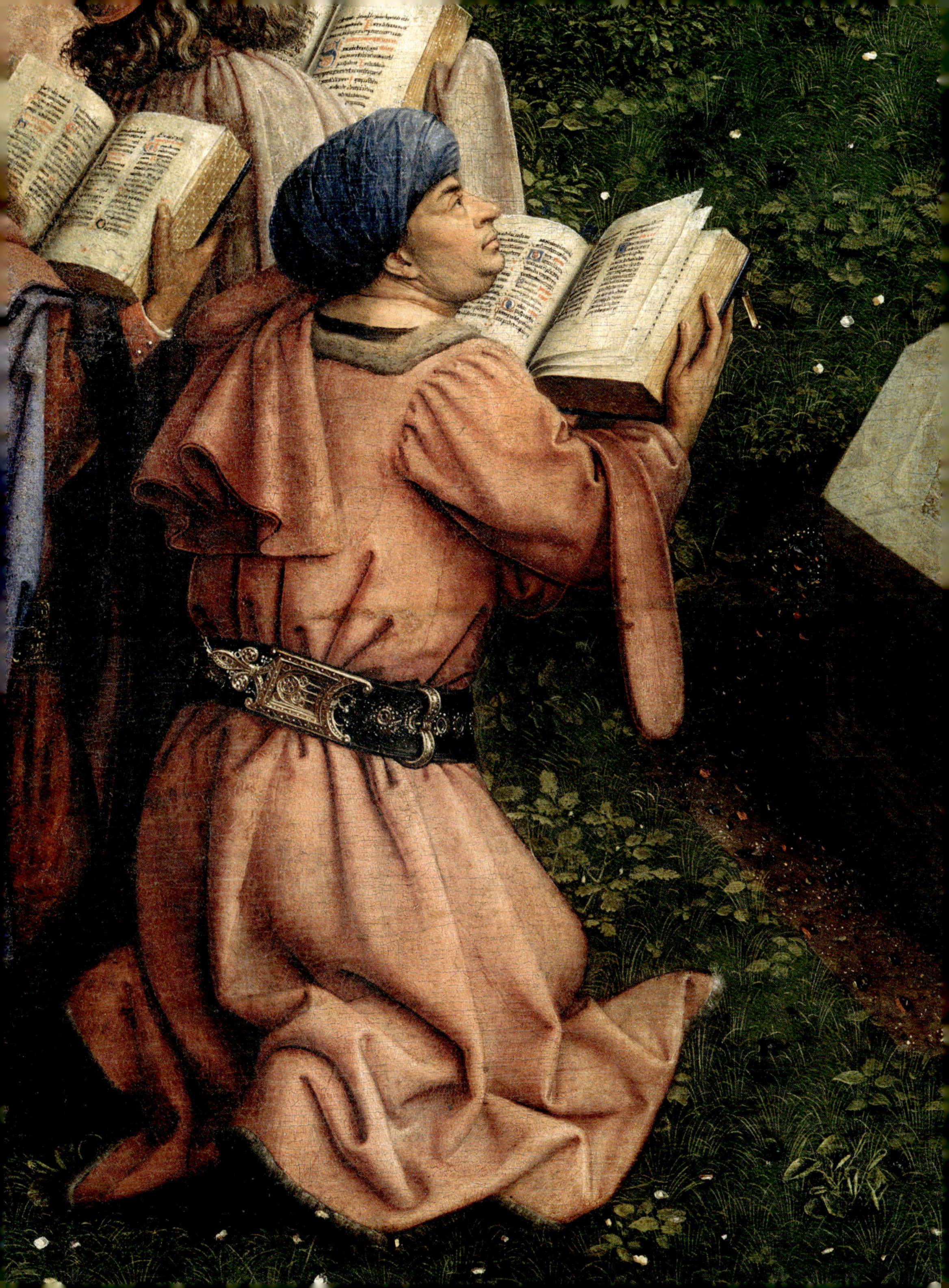

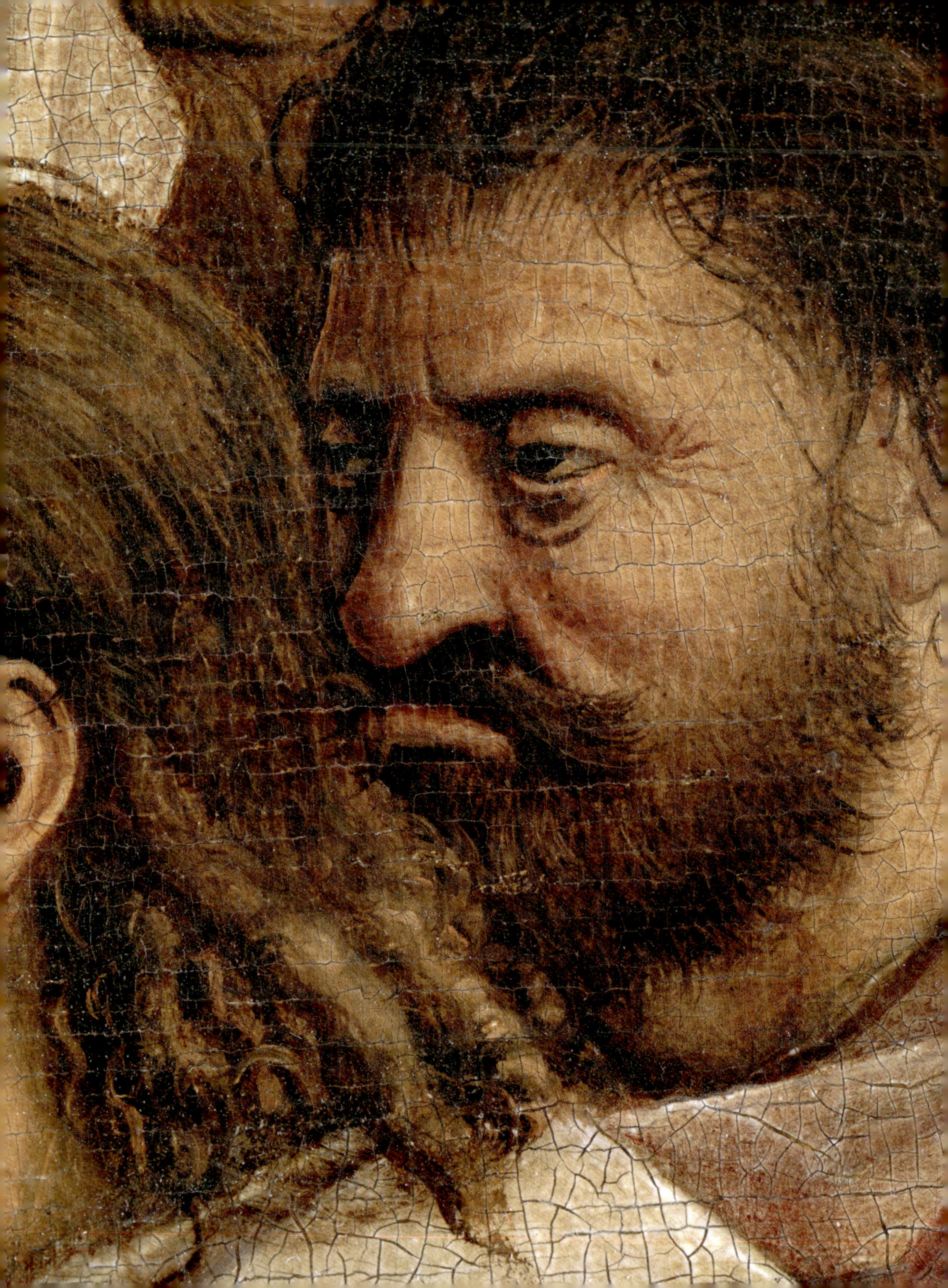

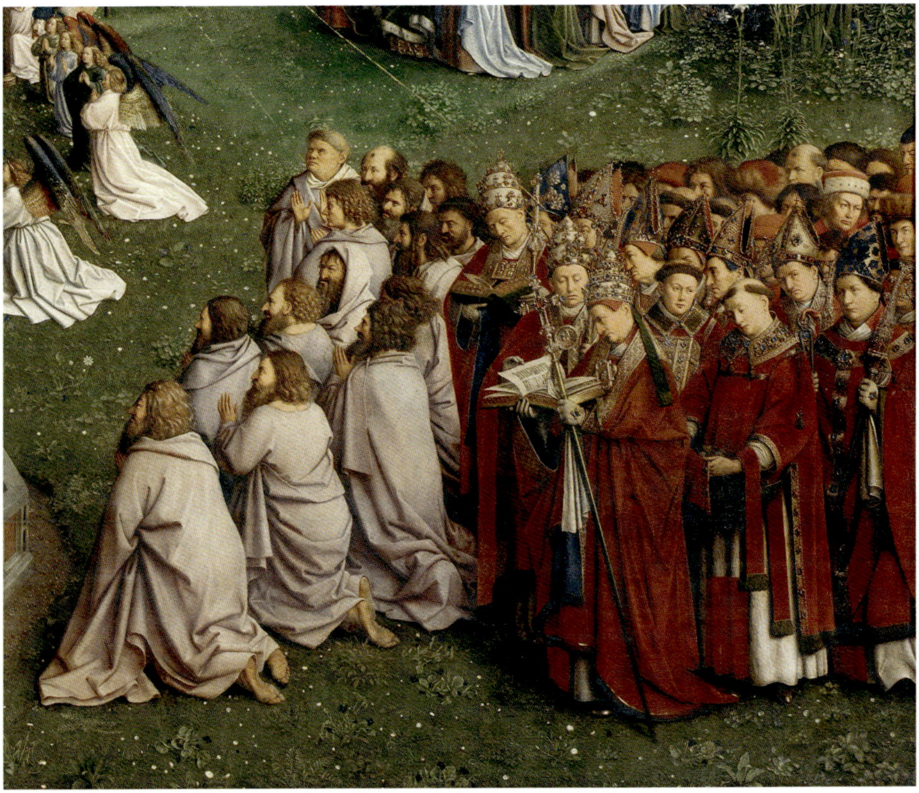

The right foreground contains a parallel group from the New Testament and the Church. The twelve Apostles are shown kneeling with Saints Paul and Barnabas – founders of the Church and the first to preach the Gospel. Behind them are three popes, six bishops and two deacons, and we also make out the heads of two monks and a number of prominent lay people. The structure of this and other groups corresponds with medieval views concerning the hierarchical structure of the world and of the Church. The red robes tell us that these are martyrs – the most important group of saints. Two of them are readily identifiable as the deacan St Stephen, who carries in his dalmatic the stones with which he was killed, and Livinus, one of Ghent's patron saints, who holds his tongue in the pincers that were used to tear it out.

Another group of Christians emerges from the bushes in the left background. We find the same hierarchical order once again – popes, cardinals, bishops (and possibly abbots), priests and monks (and possibly some lay people). Although they hold palms of victory, they are not dressed in red. These are not martyrs, therefore, but 'confessors' – saints who did not die a martyr's death.

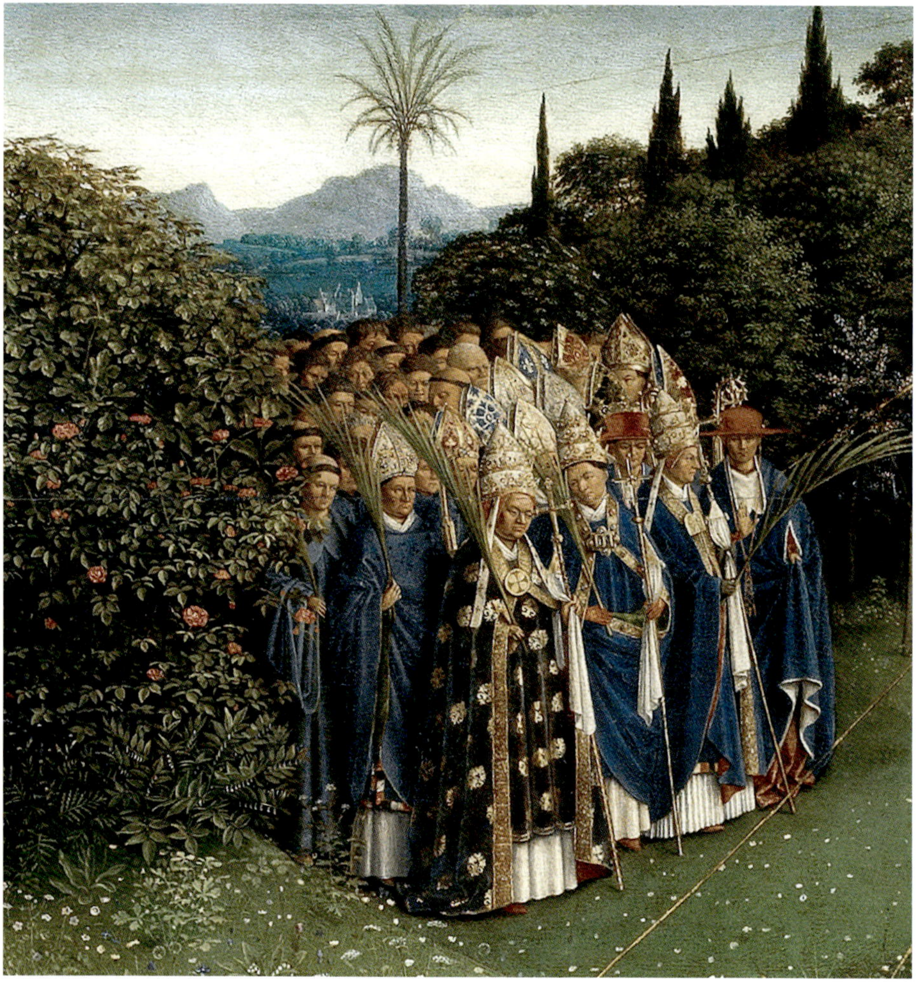

The group furthest to the right at the back is the most numerous, comprising all the female saints – martyrs and confessors alike. They are all garlanded in flowers and hold palms of victory. Several of the figures can be identified (Agnes with the lamb, Barbara with the tower, Dorothy with the basket of flowers and Ursula with the arrow). Alongside them stand all manner of anonymous women – lay and religious, including an abbess with her staff. All the women and men are dressed in costly robes as a token of their glory. Although the Book of Revelation states that the elect will all be dressed in white robes, Van Eyck has allowed himself a great deal of freedom in his interpretation of this fact.

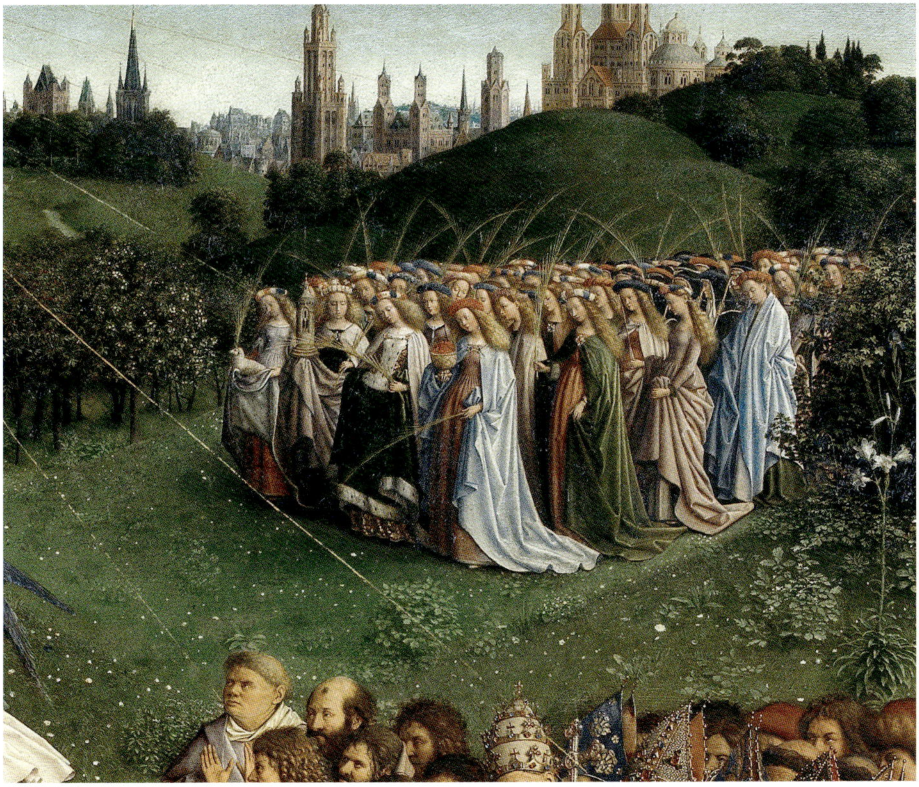

The Just Judges
The Knights of Christ

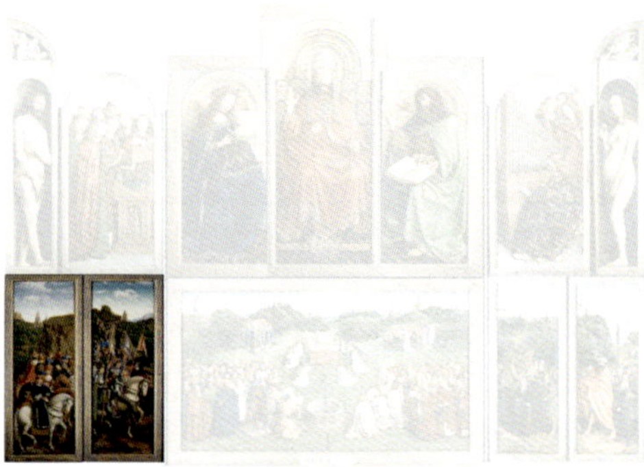

The landscape in the centre panel runs across into the wings. The groups shown in these panels are also making their way towards the central meadow to worship the Lamb. The people on the left are those of status in the world: the 'Knights of Christ' and the 'Just Judges'. The Knights of Christ were people who took up the sword in the name of Christ, according to the medieval chivalric ideal. There are several sovereigns among this group – possibly the leaders of the crusades. Some have been identified, though never conclusively, as Louis IX (St Louis), Godfrey of Bouillon and Charlemagne. The panel on the far left shows the Just Judges, who are actually administrators and politicians. This is the panel that was stolen in 1934, and what you see today is a 1939 copy by Jan Van der Veken. In spite of its quality, the attentive viewer can still spot the difference in colouring (see the rocks and the sky, for instance), while the copy also displays less depth than the originals alongside it.

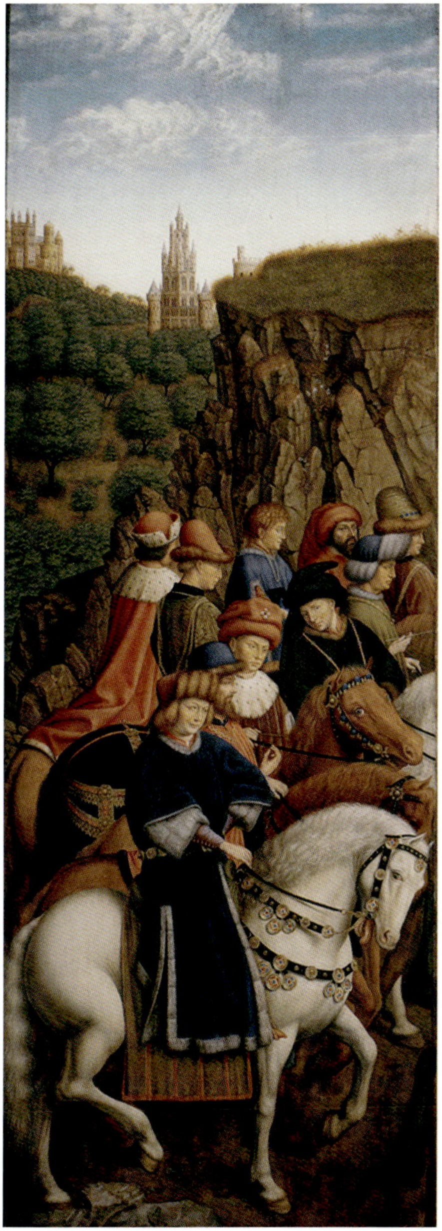
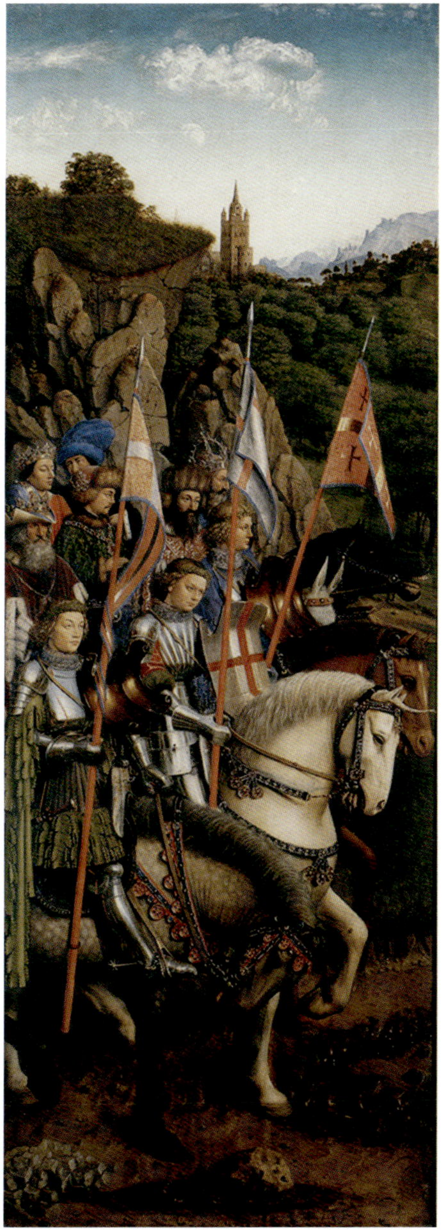

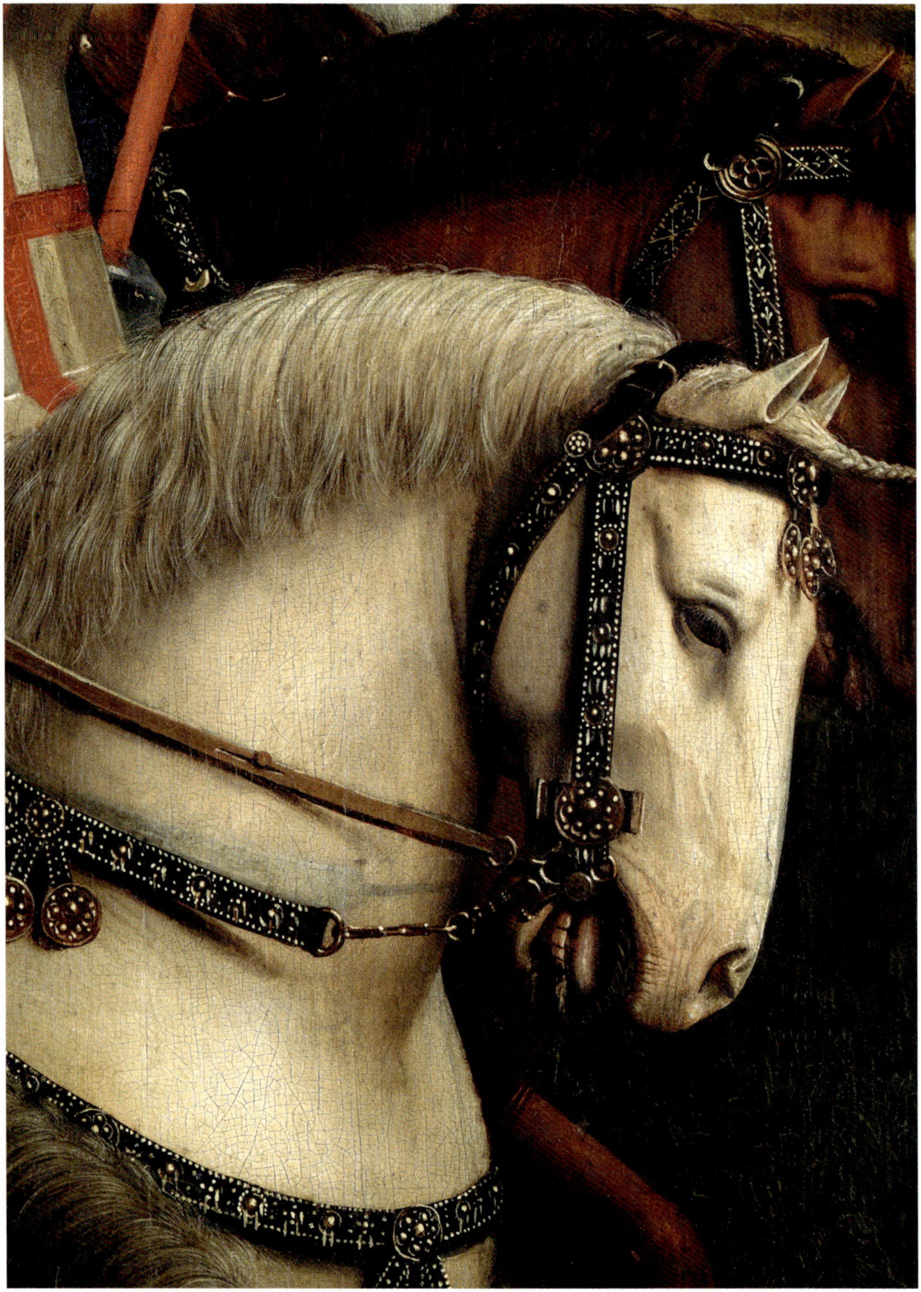

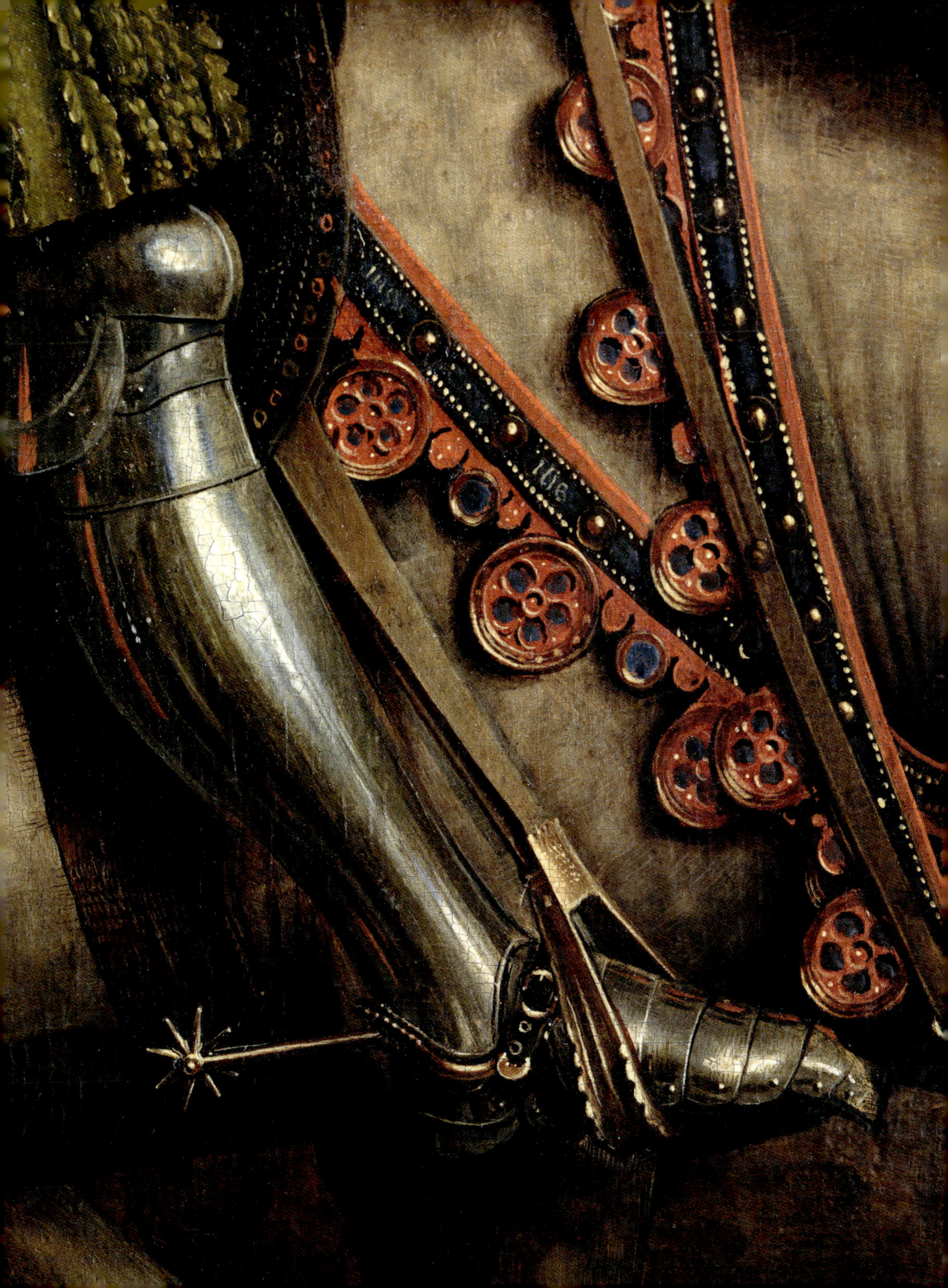

The Hermits
The Pilgrims

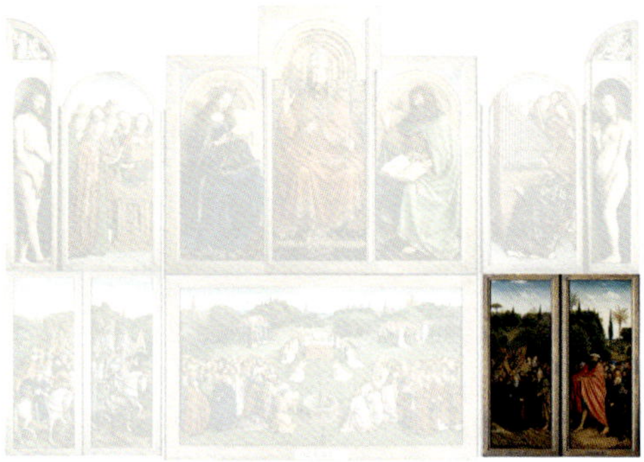

To the right of the centre panel, we find those who turned their backs on worldly pleasure in order to serve Christ. We begin with the hermits, who are joined in the background by the penitent Mary Magdalene (holding her ointment jar) and a companion. The panel on the far right is devoted to the pilgrims, who were an important feature of medieval religiosity. They are led by St Christopher, the patron saint of pilgrims and travellers and, according to his legend, a giant. At his side stands a pilgrim wearing badges from the three great pilgrimages – Compostela, Rome and Jerusalem. He might be Jodocus, patron saint of the donor. The hermits and the pilgrims are set against a beautiful Mediterranean landscape, which is one of the altarpiece's greatest glories.

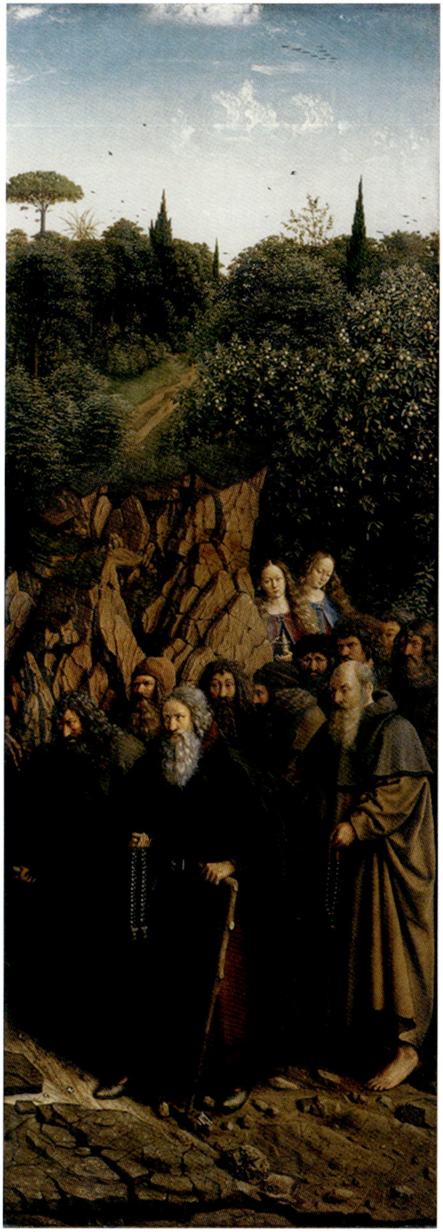

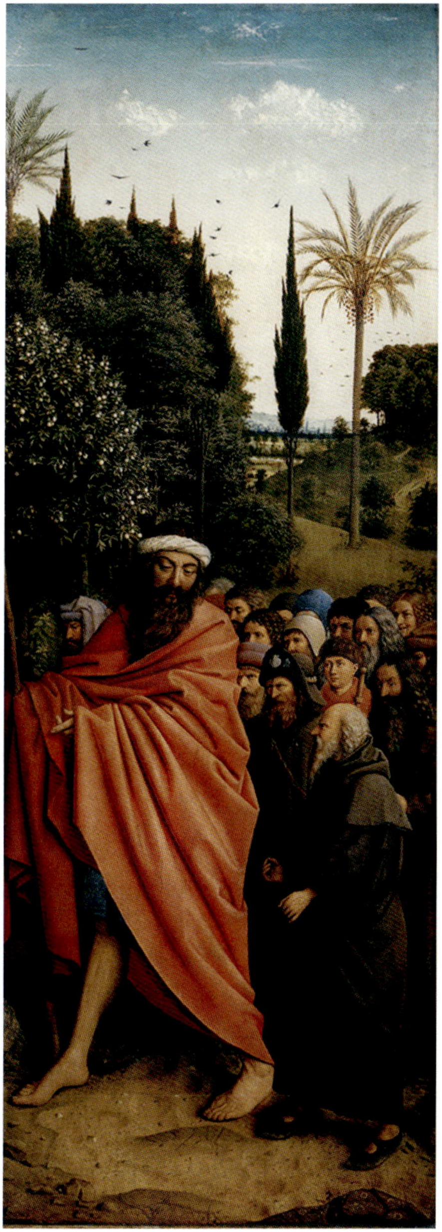

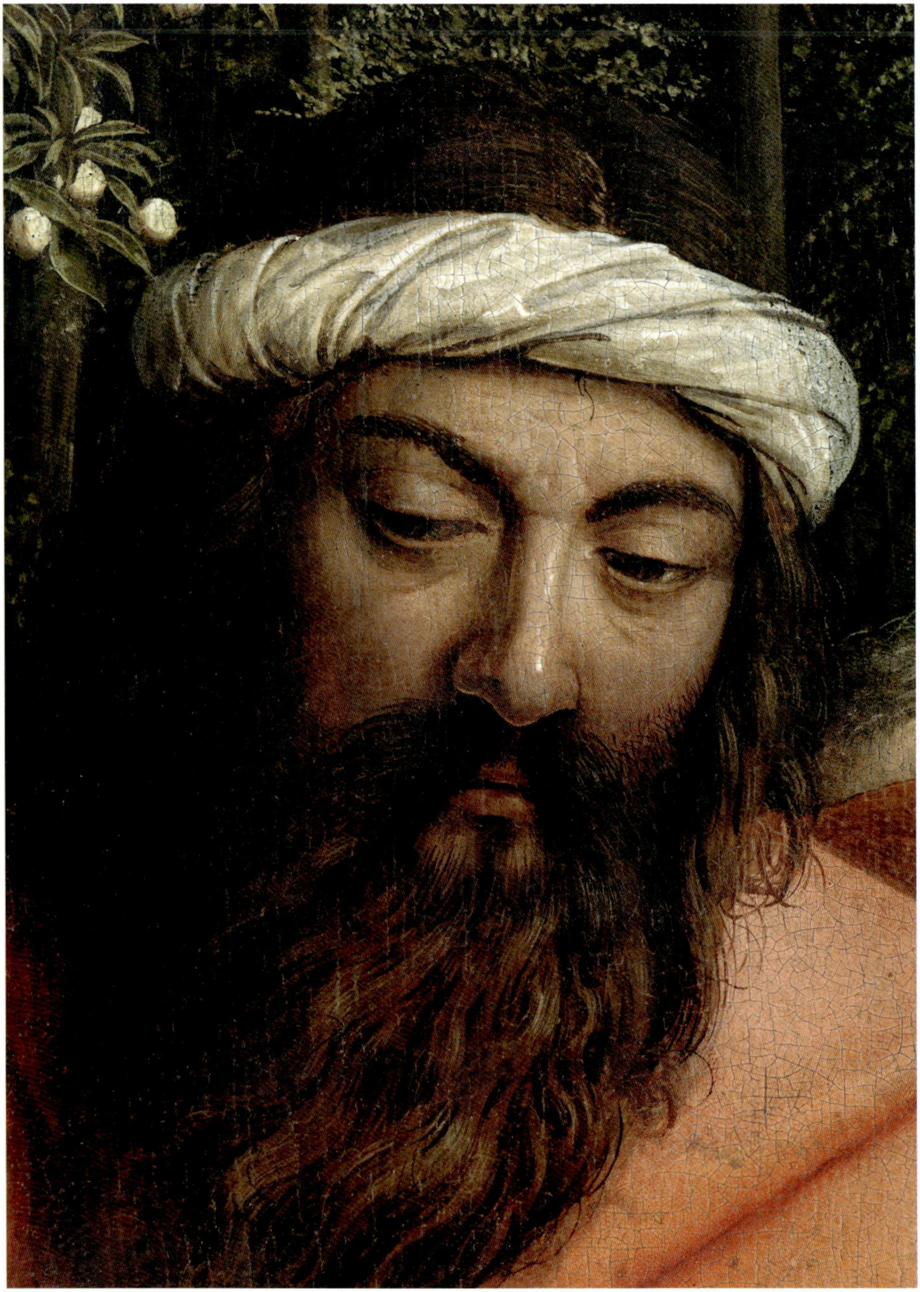

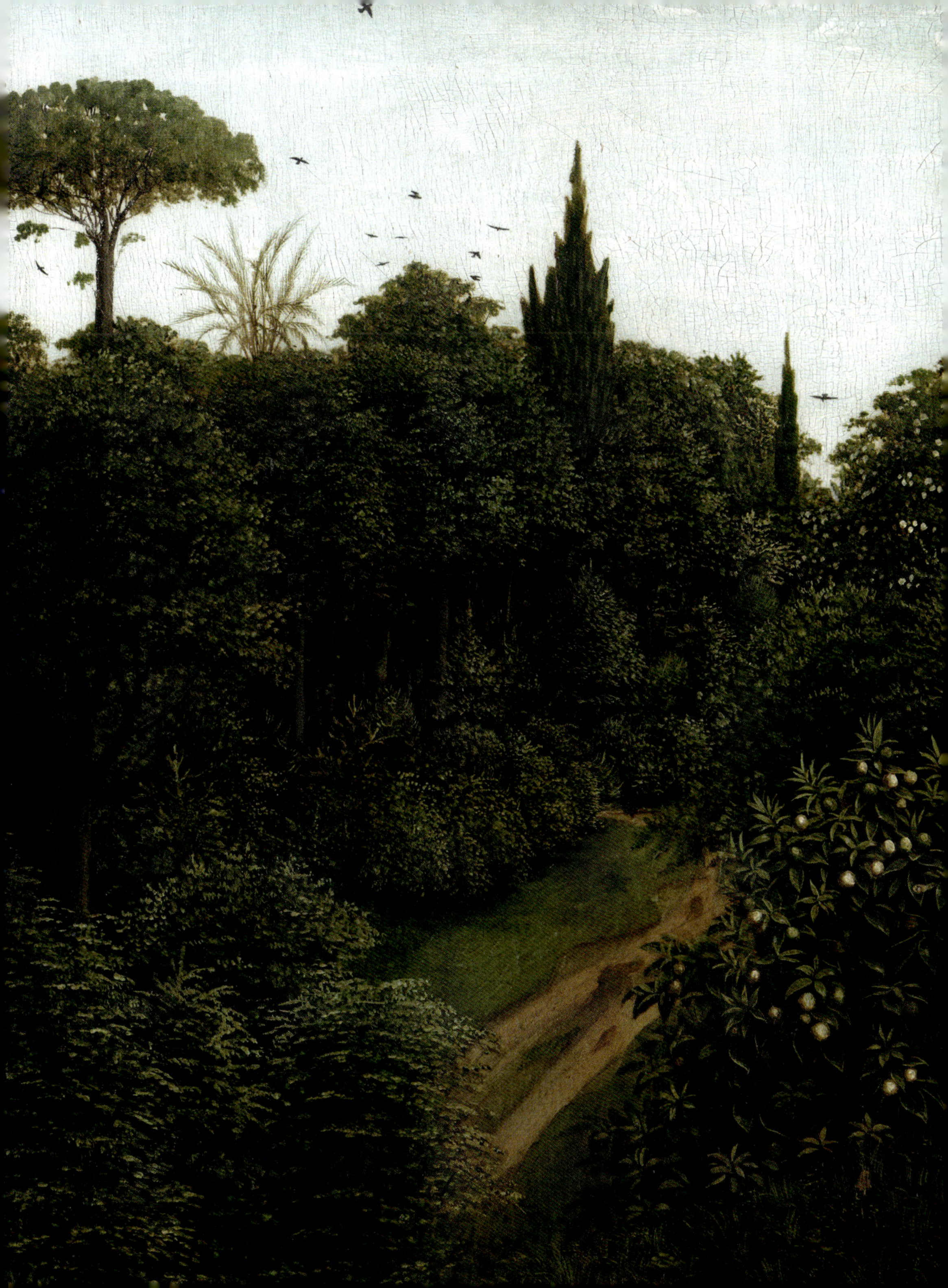

The closed altarpiece

The altarpiece used only to be opened on feast-days. For the rest of the time, the wings were closed, so that all that could be seen was the Annunciation. The colours of the open painting are deliberately brighter and more festive than those of the closed shutters. The closed altarpiece is also divided into two registers, with four separate figures in 'lunettes' at the top. X-rays have shown that the original design of the upper register was altered, possibly by Jan, during execution. Beneath the upper layer of the Annunciation, we find traces of niches like those in the lower register. Hubert's original design may well have featured saints' figures in these niches, or possibly the figures of the Annunciation. It is a pity in a way that the altarpiece can no longer be closed, as viewers are unable to see the marvellous structure of the shutters. Consequently, it is always worth looking at a model or a reproduction in which the unity of the composition can be seen.

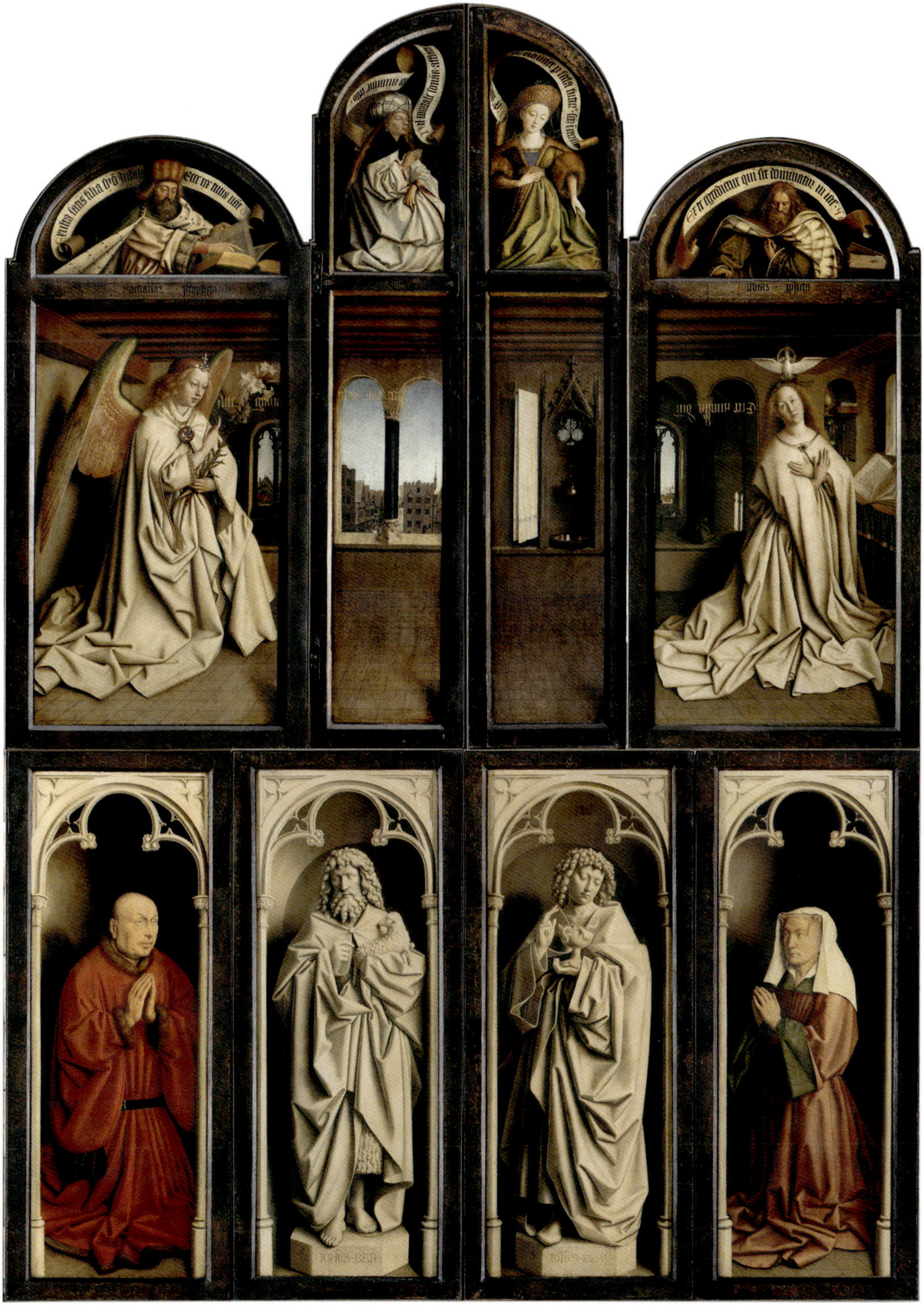

The Annunciation

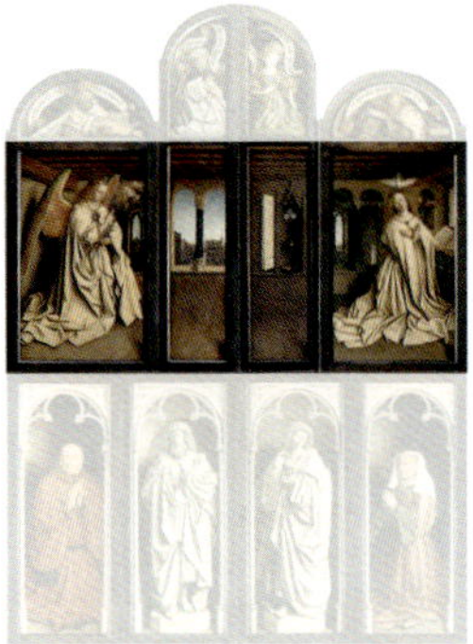

The most important scene on the closed wings is undoubtedly the one showing the Archangel Gabriel's Annunciation to Mary – a key occurrence in Christian iconography. The painter (Jan van Eyck?) has combined the four panels to form a single space, albeit one viewed from several perspectives. God's messenger appears in an attractive Flemish interior that looks out onto a street in medieval Ghent. Mary raises her eyes from her prayerbook. Gabriel, holding a lily to symbolise Mary's virginity, hails her with the words 'Greetings, most favoured one! The Lord is with you.' He brings Mary the message that the Holy Spirit of God shall descend upon her and that she will become the mother of the Messiah, the Son of God. The Holy Spirit in the guise of a dove hovers above her as she responds, 'Here am I, the servant of the Lord.' With these words, Mary affirms her commitment to God's plan, allowing the salvation of humanity through the incarnation of Christ to begin.

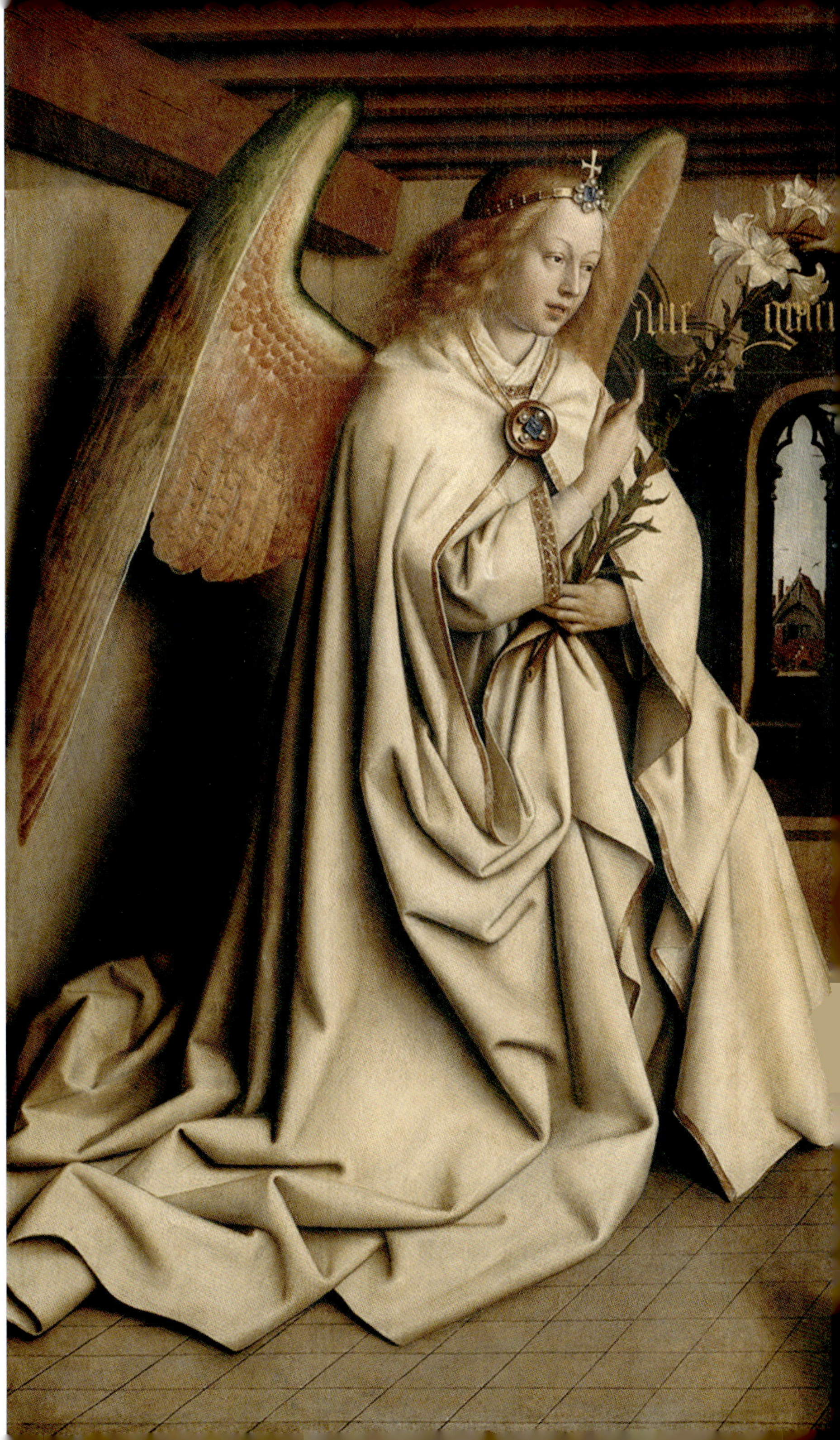

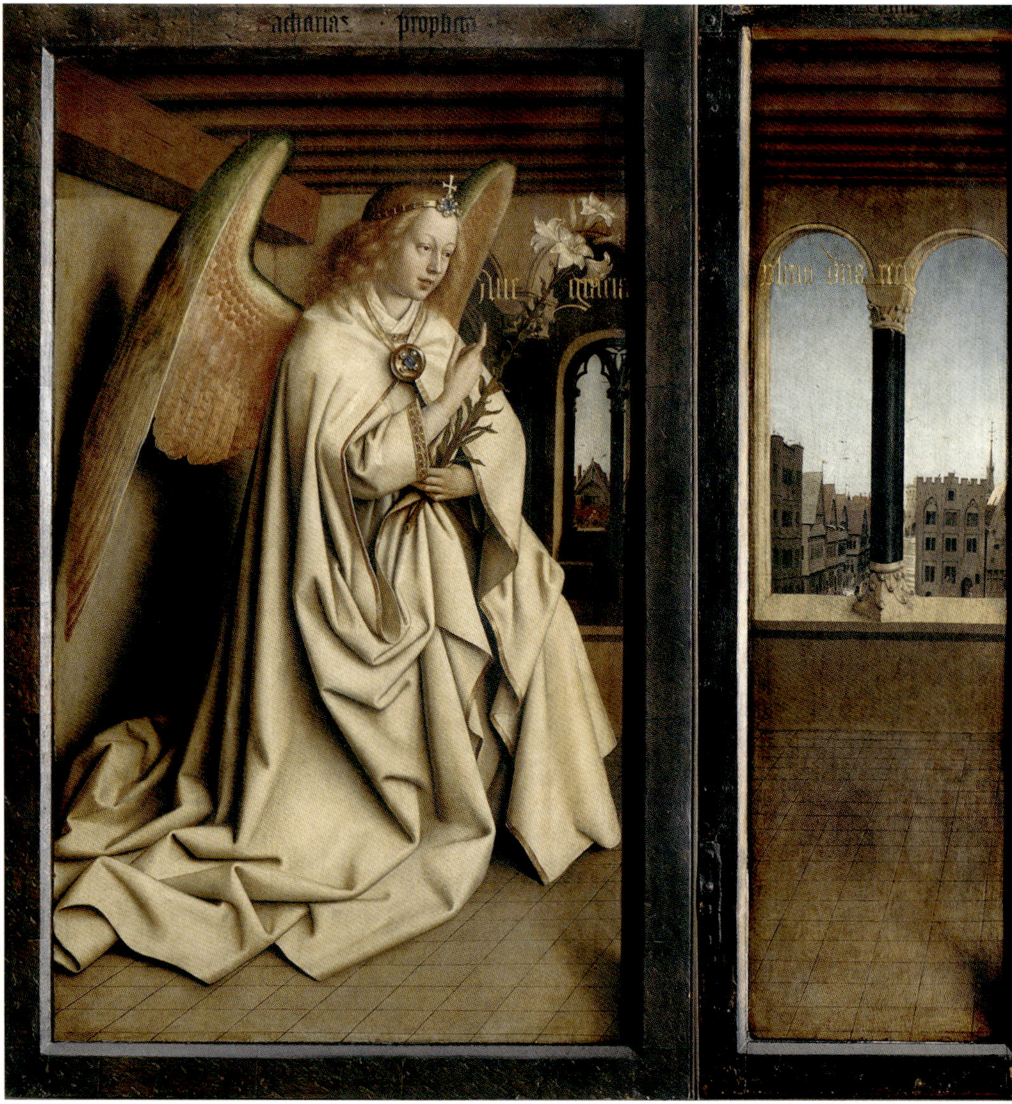

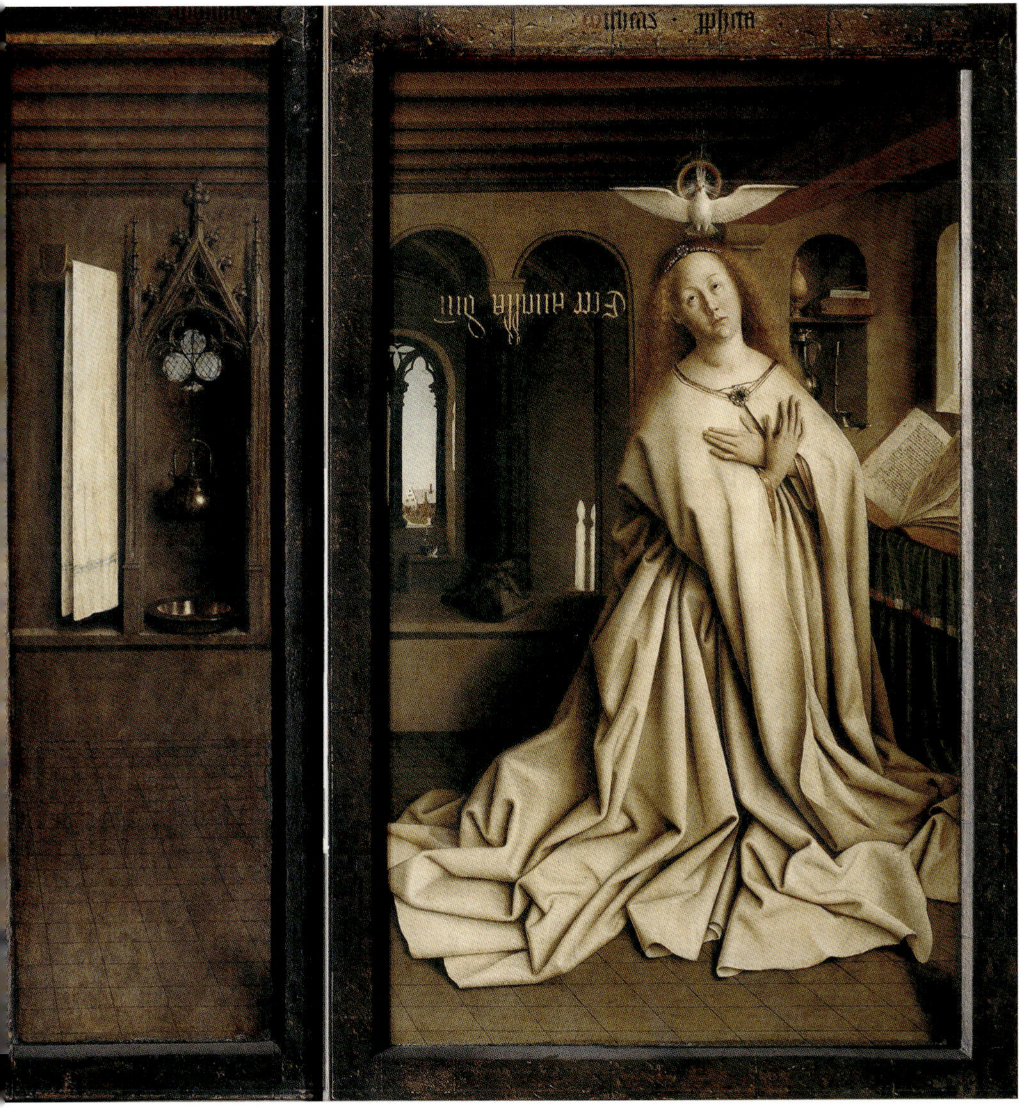

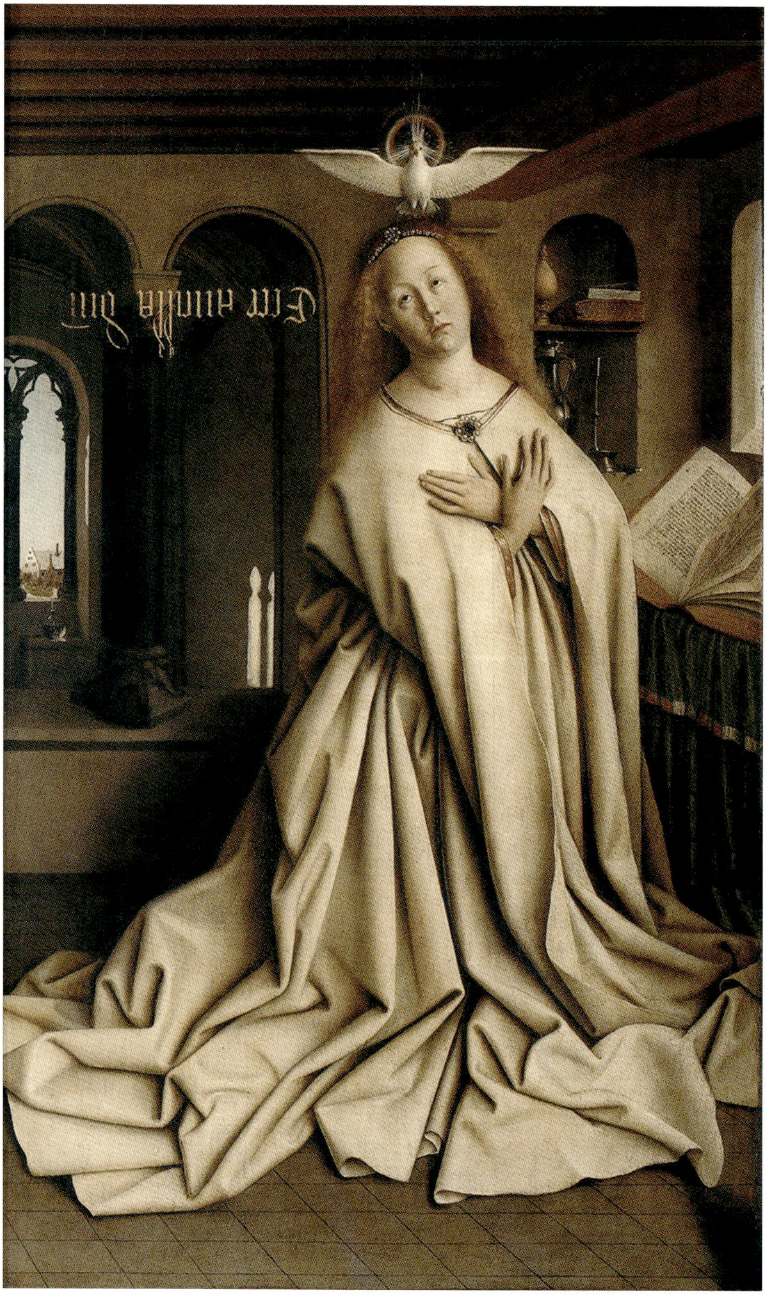

The Prophet Zacharias
The Erythrean Sibyl

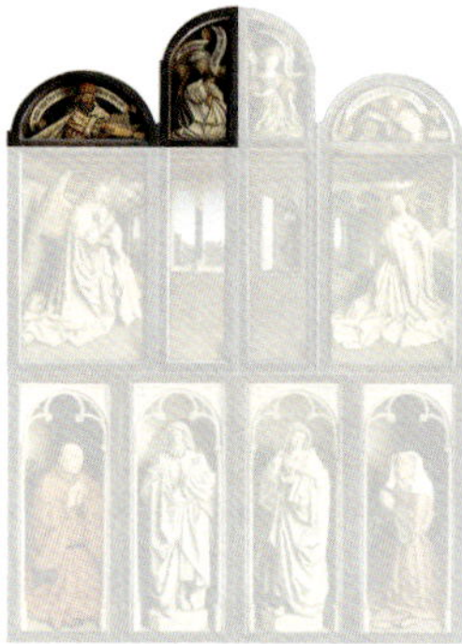

The prophet Zacharias in the lunette on the left was viewed, like Micah on the right, as one of the seers who most clearly foretold the advent of the Messiah in Bethlehem. Van Eyck chose the two to stand for the biblical prophets of Christ's birth. The Sibyl of Erythrea stands alongside Zacharias, recalling the fact that, according to medieval Christian thinking, the coming of Christ was also foreseen in the heathen world by the prophetesses known as sibyls.

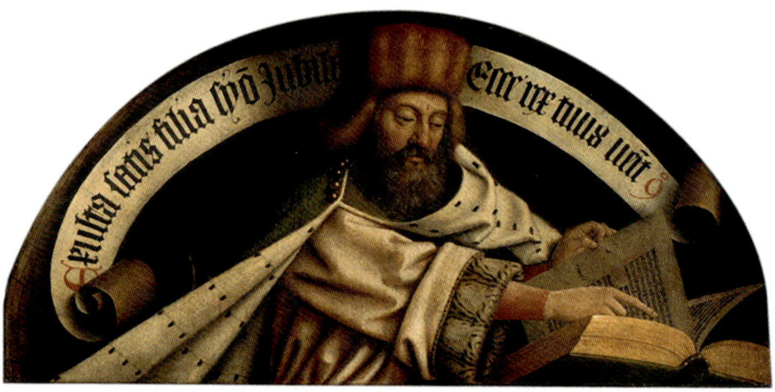

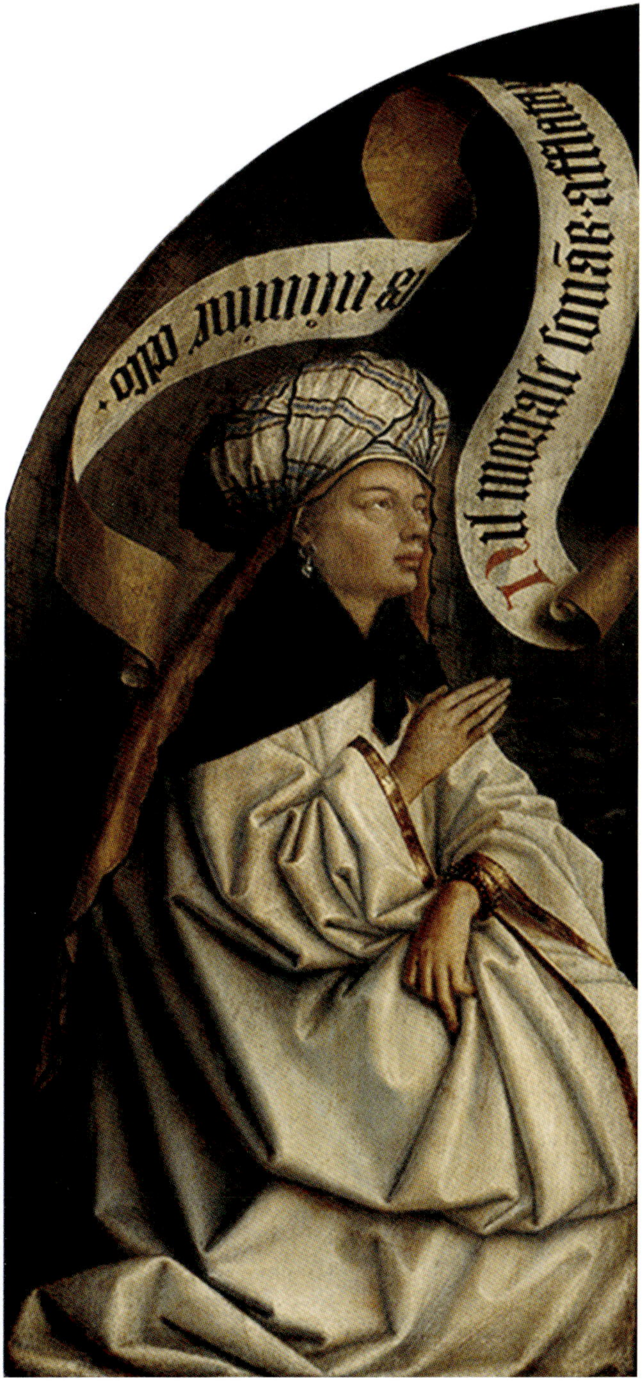

The Cumaean Sibyl
The Prophet Micah

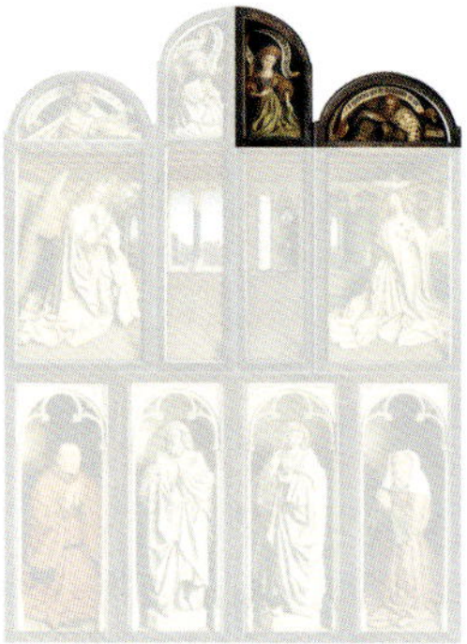

The Erythrean Sibyl is accompanied by her counterpart from Cumae, dressed in an elegant green robe, while the prophet Micah on the far right fulfils a similar balancing function for Zacharias. He looks down over the edge of his lunette at the scene below in which the Archangel Gabriel brings his message to the Virgin Mary. The latter's reply is painted upside down and from right to left, so that her acceptance is clear to the Holy Spirit and even more so to Micah.

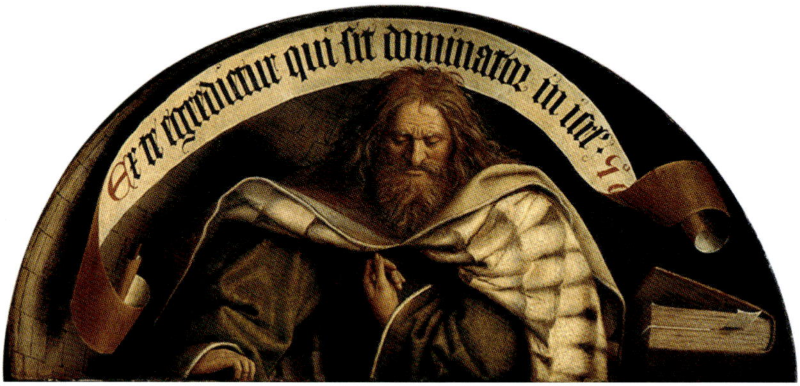

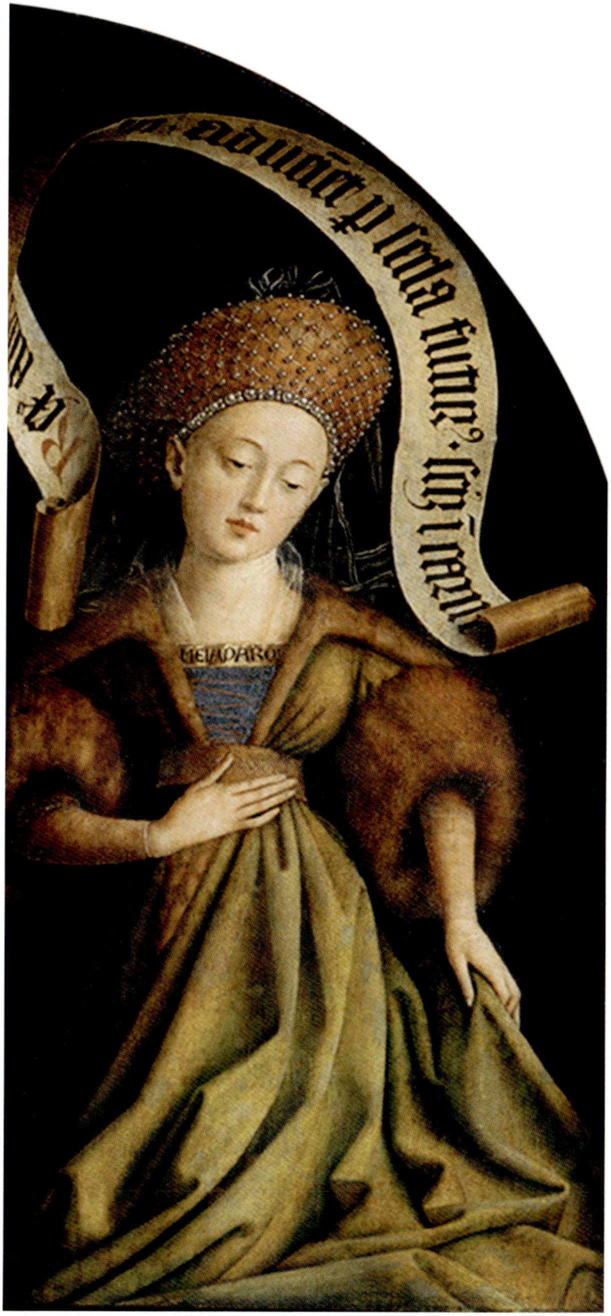

John the Baptist
John the Evangelist

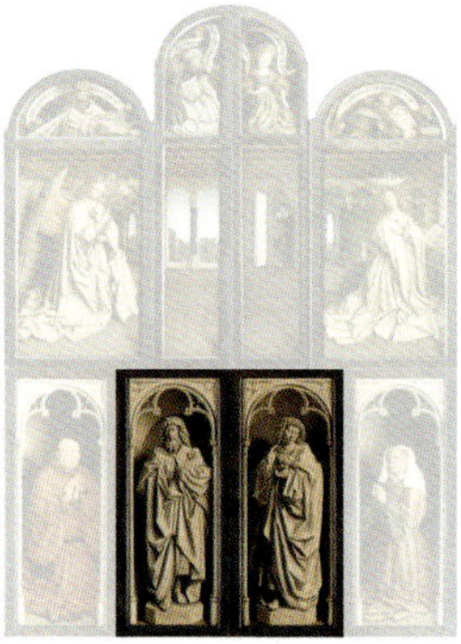

The lower register comprises four finely carved Gothic niches containing figures that do not play any part in the biblical story of the Salvation, but who were nevertheless crucial to the creation of the altarpiece. In the middle, Van Eyck painted two trompe-l'œil sandstone sculptures. They represent the two saints who figured so prominently in both the commissioning and content of the work. On the left we see John the Baptist, who is clearly identifiable from the Lamb, which he traditionally holds under his arm and points to with his finger. As the patron saint of the Church of St John, his presence in the altarpiece is self-evident. The young man next to him is the Apostle John – writer of one of the four Gospels and traditionally identified as the author of the 'Revelation of John' or the Apocalypse. The name 'Lamb of God' comes from his Gospel, while the entire liturgy of the worship of the Lamb – including the symbols of the heavenly Jerusalem and the Fountain of Life – derive from the Apocalypse. His presence in the painting is, therefore, entirely natural. John the Evangelist is shown holding a chalice containing poisonous adders. The image refers to an early legend, in which John is said to have drunk from a poisoned cup yet survived.

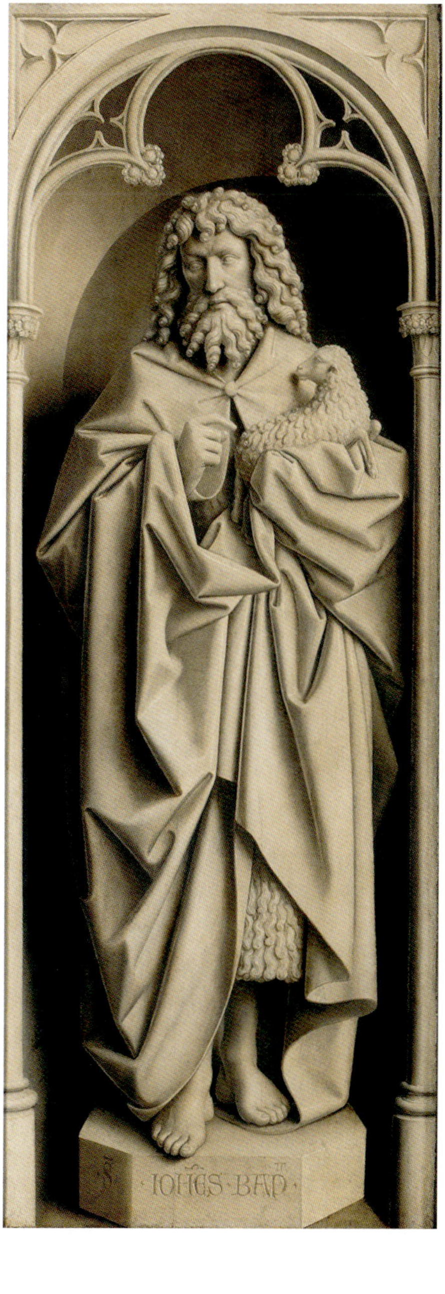
IOHES·BAP

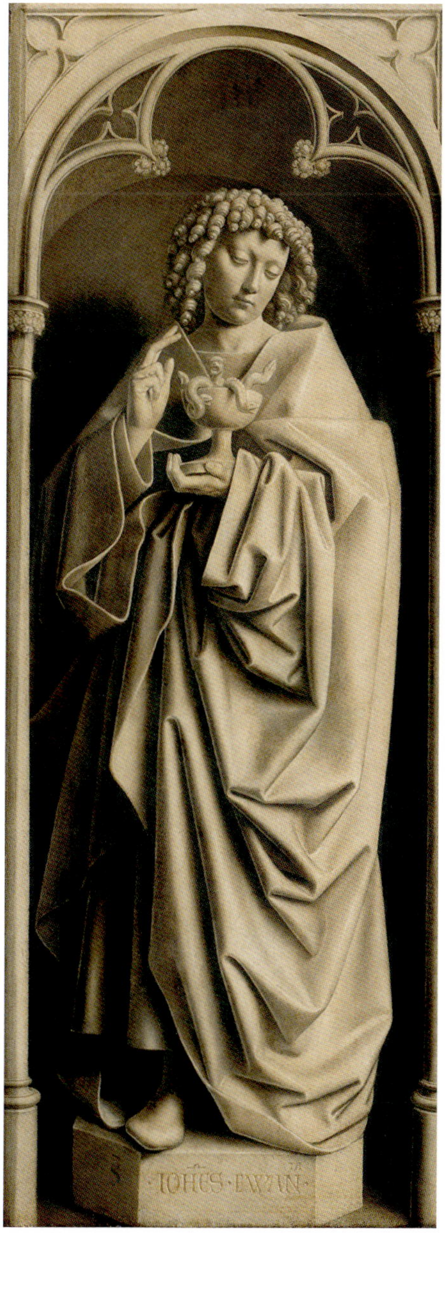
IOHES·EWAN

Jodocus Vyd
Elizabeth Borluut

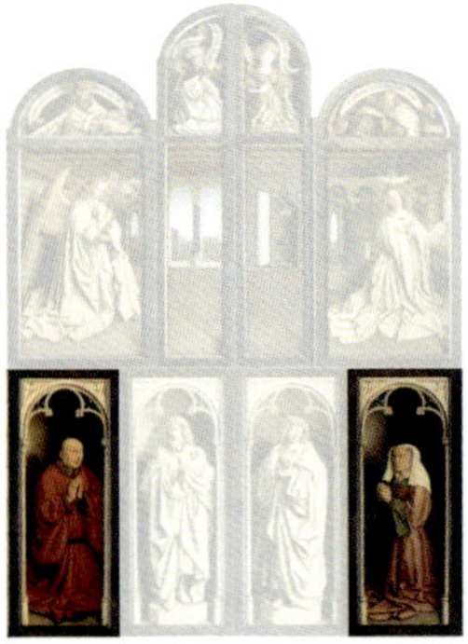

The donors of this masterpiece were also given a well-deserved place in the lower register. Jan van Eyck was an exceptionally talented portrait painter, remarkable for the way he never flattered his sitters but captured them with an unflinching, realistic gaze. The figures of Jodocus Vyd and Elizabeth Borluut are no exception. Kneeling in prayer, they are dressed in plain but expensive cloth. Six centuries later, they piously watch over this marvellous work that the world owes to their generosity.

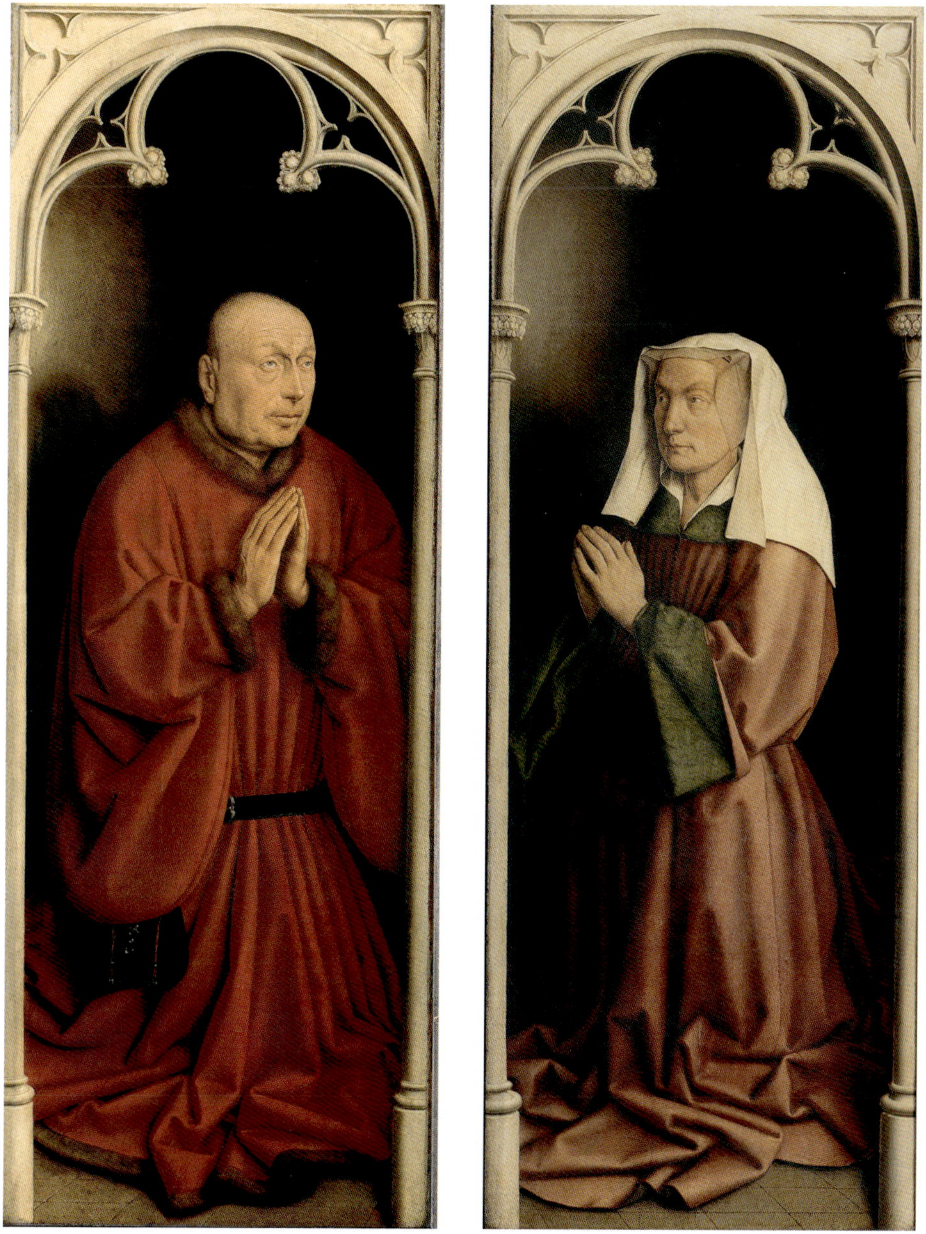

– 6 –

INTERPRETATION OF THE ICONOGRAPHY

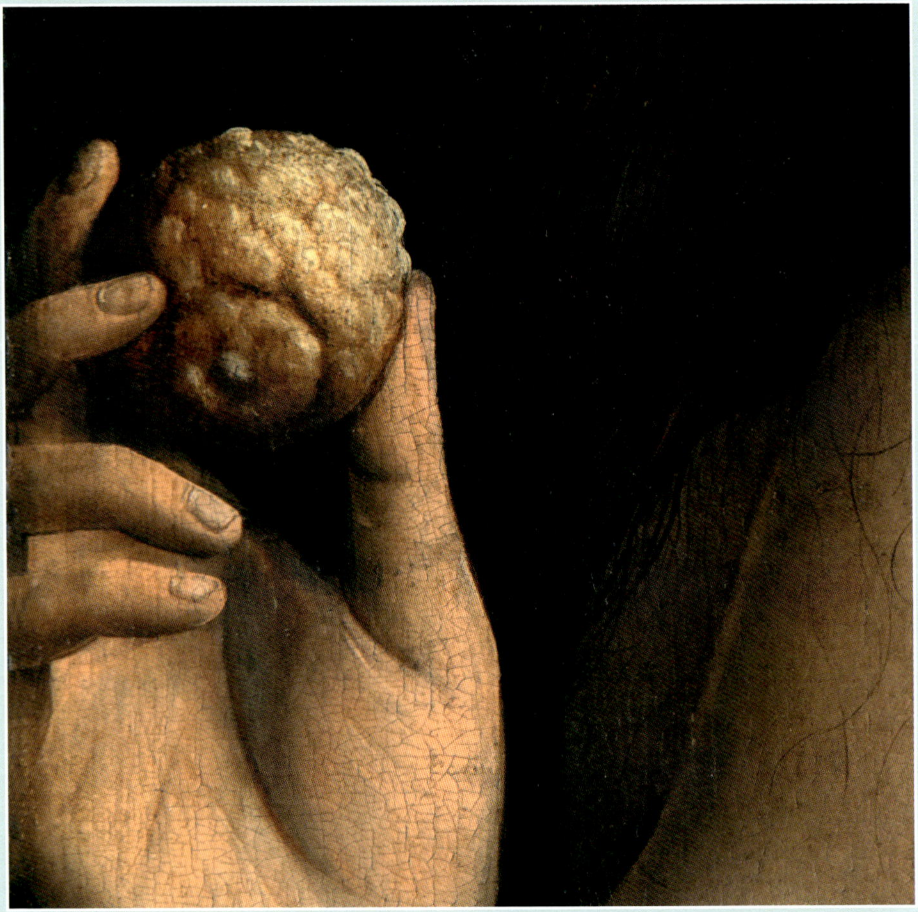

What was the purpose of the Ghent Altarpiece?

The medieval painters and sculptors of religious works did not produce images purely for beauty's sake. Aesthetic value was a secondary consideration, brought to bear on behalf of the primary goal, which was to communicate an important element of Christian belief. Artists in the Middle Ages did not view their creations as 'works of art' in the sense that we understand today. They hoped through their work to serve God and the Church, and to help disseminate and strengthen the ideas that together constituted the Christian faith. The aesthetic aspect was a means rather than an end in itself. Works of art were intended as a gift in honour of God and as a tool by which to educate and edify. Although the polyptych was produced on the threshold of the Renaissance, which saw a gradual shift in these views, it still strongly reflects its theological and catechistic purposes. The notion of abstract or themeless painting would have been incomprehensible to the artists of that period. The purpose of the altarpiece was, therefore, to serve God and the Church by illustrating several key elements of Christian faith.

Christ's redemption of humanity

The principal theme of the altarpiece is clearly the *Salvation of humanity*. Christianity is essentially a religion of redemption with, as its ultimate goal, the liberation of humankind from evil in all its forms.

The biblical tradition on which the Christian and Jewish faiths are based, displays a keen awareness of evil. Biblical history begins in the Book of Genesis in an atmosphere of tragedy (Genesis is the first book of the Bible – one of the 66 texts or 'books' that make up the Old and New Testaments). God's creation of the world is full of optimism, as God 'saw that it was good' and blessed his creation. Things began to go wrong, however, from the very beginning of human history, as people abused the freedom they had been given. The Bible thus expresses a tragic sense that humanity has been marked by suffering and pain throughout its existence. Moreover, all forms of evil merely foreshadow the inescapable endpoint of death.

The Bible does not express this universal sense in philosophical language, but through a mythological story. The first human beings – Adam ('man') and Eve ('mother of all living beings') – were called into existence as innocent as children, pure in their nakedness. Eve, however, immediately allowed herself to be tempted into disobeying God by the serpent, symbol of evil and later of Satan. The serpent persuaded Eve to eat the 'fruit of the knowledge of good and evil', so that she could become God's equal. Things were to turn out entirely differently – the instant she and Adam tasted the fruit, they became aware of their nakedness and were ashamed, covering themselves with fig leaves and attempting to hide from God. The latter's response was to punish them and their descendants. No more living in paradise – henceforth, humanity would live a life of affliction and pain. Men and women would have to sweat to till the soil, men would have dominion over women and new life would only be born in pain. And all this would end in death, with a reminder to all people that they were nothing but dust and that to dust they would return. In this way, the Bible explains the many forms of pain and evil in the world as God's punishment for the sins of humanity. Given that all people were believed to be marked by sin, which was literally passed down from one generation to another, the Christian Church later spoke of 'Original Sin'. The Bible makes plain the consequences of this sin shortly after Adam and Eve's banishment from the Garden of Eden, when Cain – the first human child to be conceived – was prompted by jealousy to murder his brother, Abel. In other words, human history got off to a pretty gloomy start.

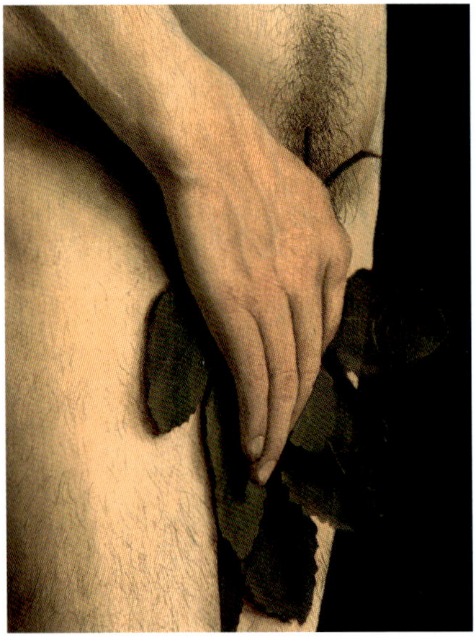

Van Eyck shows all of this in the altarpiece: Eve holding the bitter fruit of the

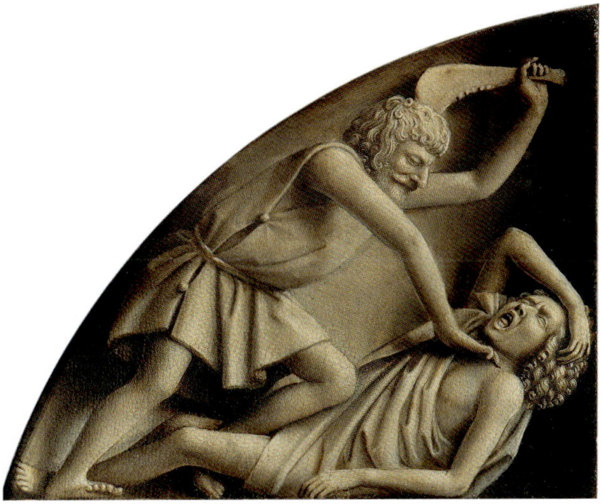

The ass's jawbone comes from the story of Samson, who used such a bone to kill thousands of Philistines. Its use in this context is a piece of artistic licence – Van Eyck may have seized on it because, according to the Bible, the first humans had no weapons. It was the descendants of Cain who began to forge them.

tree, Adam on the other side and, above them, the story of Cain and Abel in the form of a stone relief: Cain slays his brother above Eve's head using the jawbone of an ass. Biblical history does not cease, however, with this tragic opening tale. The religion expounded in the Bible is one of hope. The prospect of redemption from evil is raised right from the outset. In a sense, biblical history in all its immensity boils down to the recurrent rise of evil and periods of great suffering, invariably followed by liberation. No matter how unfaithful people prove to be, God is always true to his covenant with humanity.

During a later period of biblical Judaism, the belief arose that God would redeem the world by sending a saviour, who was conceived in terms of a king. The Hebrew word 'Messiah' and the Greek 'Christos' both translate as 'anointed one', reflecting the fact that kings were anointed with oil during their coronation. That brings us to the threshold of Christian belief, which is wholly rooted in the tragedy and hope of the Jewish Bible. Where Christians differ from Jews, is in their belief that God has already sent the redeemer of humanity, in the person of Jesus of Nazareth, which is why they refer to Jesus as 'the Messiah' and as 'Christ'.

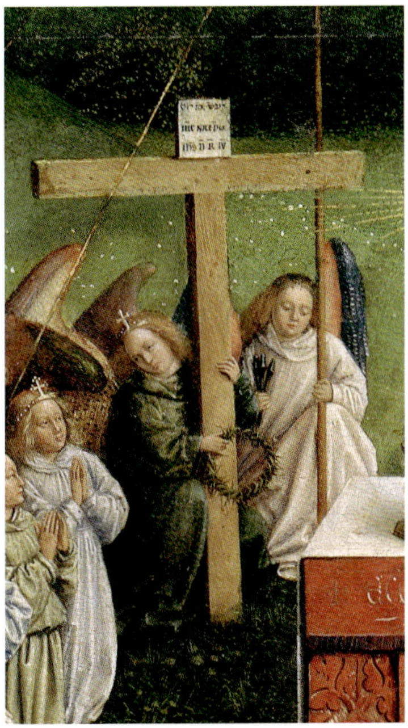

The Roman authorities crucified the historical Jesus around the year 30. His disciples began shortly afterwards to spread the 'Good News' that Jesus had risen from the dead and now sat in glory at God's right hand. Jesus' death on the cross was interpreted as a loving sacrifice on behalf of all sinners. By giving his life for humanity, Jesus overcame evil and mortality, conquered sin and death, and gave people the hope of redemption and eternal life. Following the drama of the lost paradise, the hope was created of a new and lasting paradise beyond the threshold of death.

As part of this belief, Christians proclaimed Jesus Christ as the 'Son of God', who became human through God's mercy. The moment at which he is received into his mother's womb was thus traditionally taken as the beginning of humanity's salvation and given an important place in the Christian tradition. Luke described the

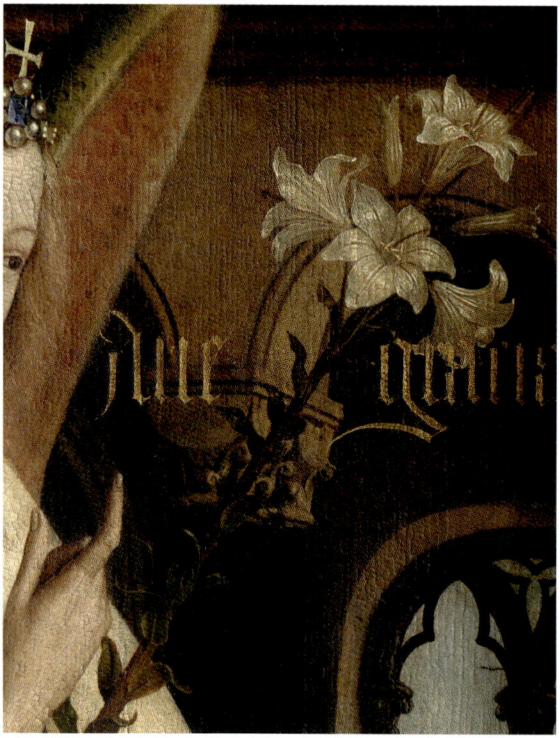

moment as follows in his Gospel: a messenger from God – the Archangel Gabriel – was sent to Mary to tell her that she was to be the mother of the Messiah and to seek her co-operation. To emphasise the holy nature of the event and the exclusivity of God's work, Christian tradition has always held that Mary remained a virgin. The Saviour was not conceived by man and woman together, but was placed in the womb by the creative power of God himself, referred to in the Bible as the 'Holy Spirit'. The latter is traditionally represented as a dove, which is probably a reference to the divine origins of the spirit. The symbol of Mary's virginity is one of the best-loved themes in Christian devotion – in the Orthodox tradition even more so than in the Catholic. Paintings and sculptures contain numerous symbols of her purity, including lilies, carafes of water with sunbeams passing through them and the three stars on her robe.

Unsurprisingly perhaps, Christians gradually began to reinterpret the Old Testament as preparing the way for the advent of Christ. A variety of Old Testament texts were read as prophesying the birth of the Messiah, which explains why biblical prophets appeared regularly in paintings and sculptures. There are two in Van Eyck's altarpiece. But the redeemer was not an exclusively Jewish figure – prophecies concerning the birth of the Messiah also appear in classical pagan texts, in which they were frequently attributed to prophetesses known as sibyls, of whom Van Eyck also includes two in his painting. By way of comparison, Michelangelo's Sistine Chapel contains seven prophets and four sibyls.

The Christians themselves added several texts to what they considered Holy Scripture. The best known of these are the four Gospels recounting the life of Jesus. These, combined with a number of other texts, form the New Testament, the most striking and strangest book of which is the final one – the Revelation of John. Also known from the Greek as the 'Apocalypse', the book comprises a series of surreal visions in which the author foresees the final stages of human history. Against a background of horrific natural disasters, the forces of evil come together to persecute and exterminate God's chosen people. Once again, however, there is an undertone of hope and joy in the book – while persecution and catastrophe hold the world in their grip, the author also offers a series of visions of Heaven. It is clear from these that the conquest of evil has already been achieved through the sacrifice of Christ – the Lamb of God. A divine liturgy is developed around the figure of the Lamb to celebrate the final victory over sin and death. This is the liturgy that Van Eyck presents in the lower register of the opened altarpiece, which takes place against the background of an imaginary city – the heavenly Jerusalem that also derives from the Book of Revelation.

In a sense, the Adoration of the Lamb altarpiece is a synthesis of the story of the Salvation, beginning with the tragedy of the sinful first humans and the first fratricide, and moving through prophecies of the Messiah's coming to the actual announcement of Jesus' birth. The climax comes with the symbolic presentation of Christ's sacrifice as the bleeding lamb on the altar and the glorious redemption of humanity represented by this heavenly liturgy. All watched over, of course, by God, the Virgin Mary, St John the Baptist and the angels who sing and play their divine music. It is unclear whether the artists or the priests who advised the painter(s) deliberately formulated this coherent, overarching theme. However, all the elements we see in the altarpiece are clearly linked to the story of the Salvation as recounted in the Bible and in wider Christian thought.

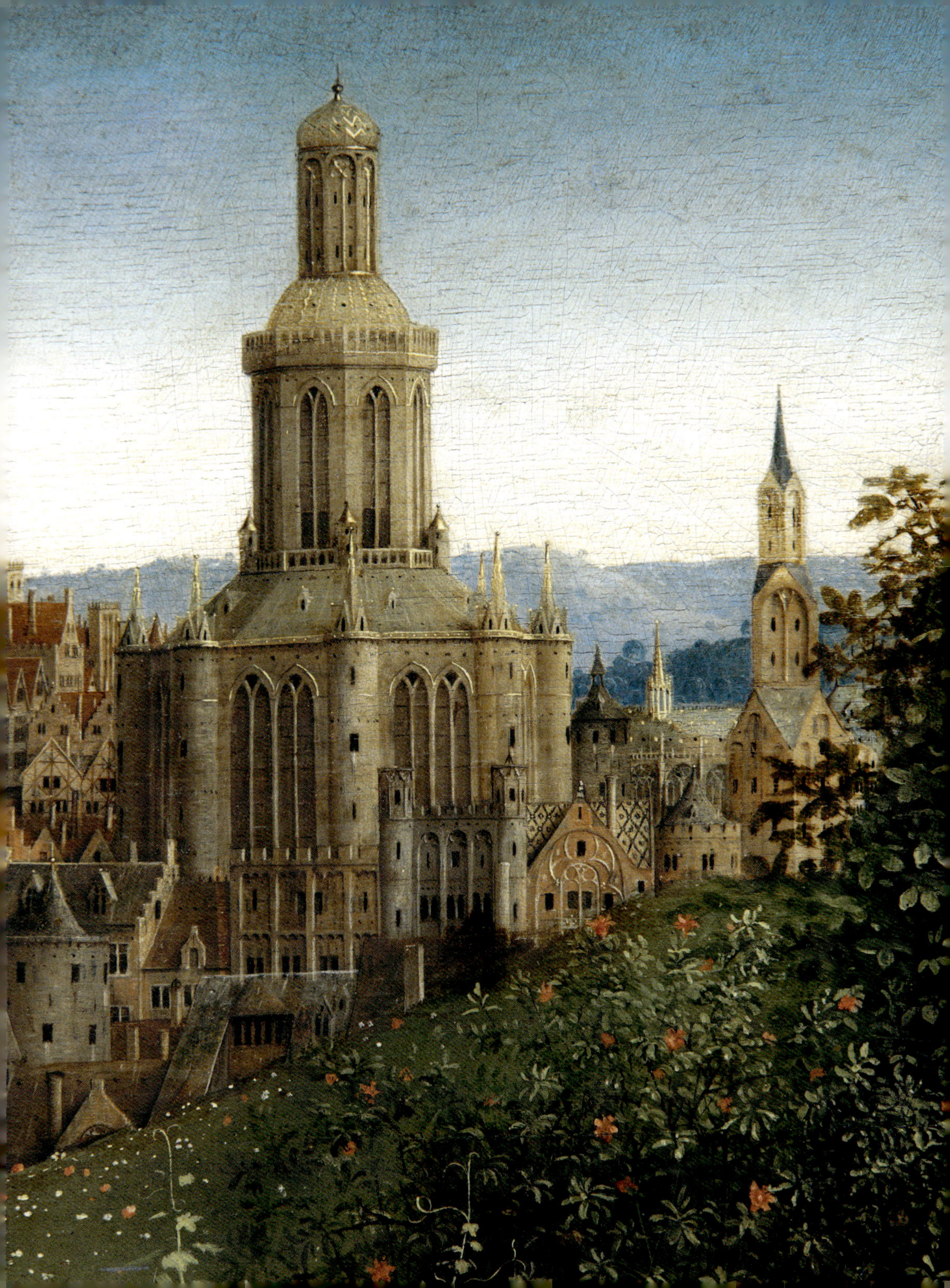

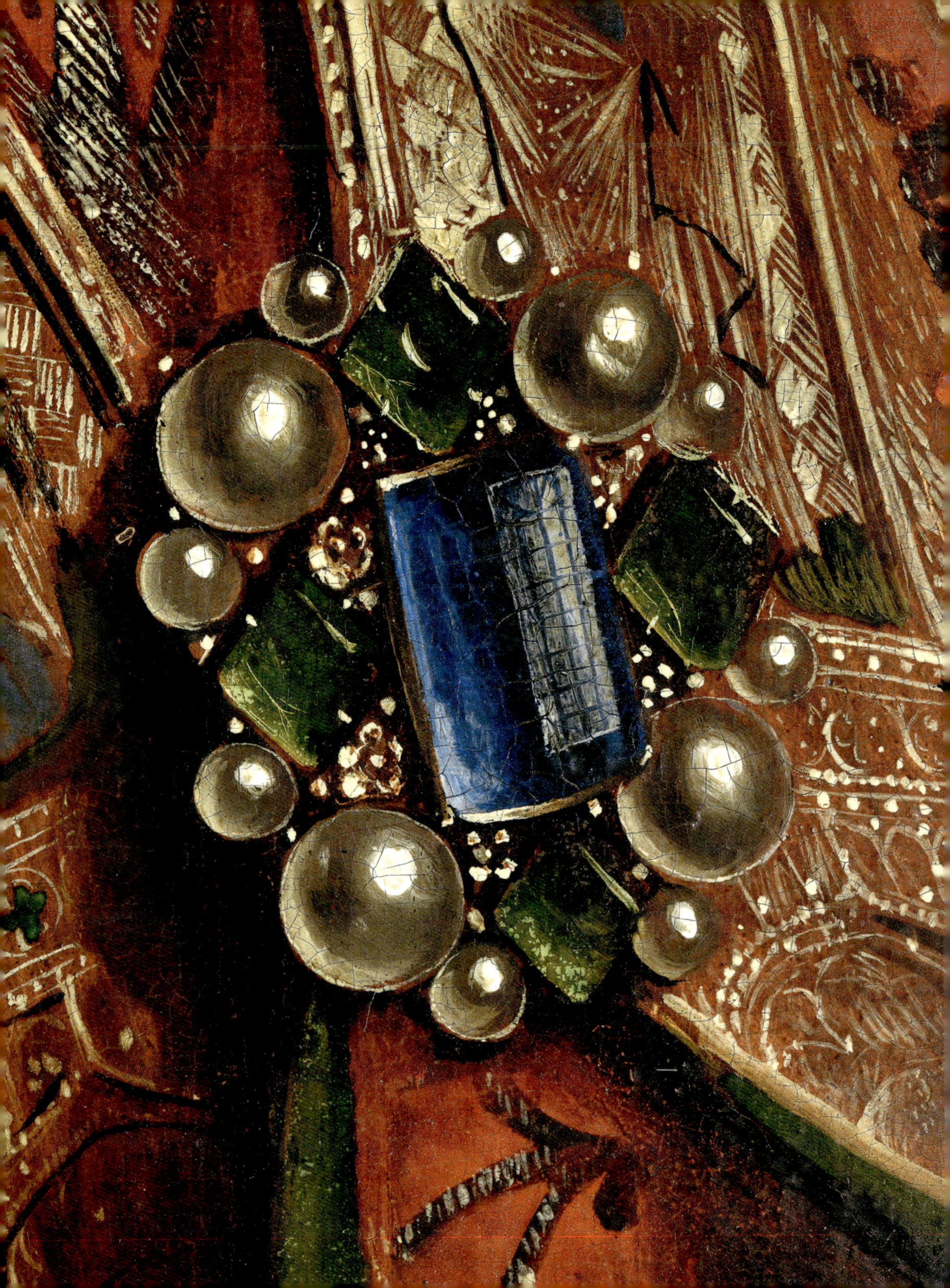

BIBLIOGRAPHY

Till-Holger Borchert, *Jan Van Eyck*, Cologne, Taschen, 2008.

Annick Born, Maximiliaan P.J. Martens, *Van Eyck in detail*, Antwerp, Ludion, 2012.

Pim W.F. Brinkman e.a., *Het Lam Godsretabel van Van Eyck: een heronderzoek naar de materialen en de schildermethoden, I. De plamuur, de isolatielaag, de tekening en de grondtonen*, in: Bulletin de l'Institut Royal du Patrimoine Artistique, XX (1984–85), pp. 137–166.

Albert Châtelet, *Hubert et Jan Van Eyck, créateurs de l'Agneau Mystique*, Dijon, Ed. Faton, 2011.

P. Coremans, A. Janssens de Bisthoven, *The Adoration of the Mystic Lamb*, Amsterdam-Antwerp, 1948.

J. De Baets, *De gewijde teksten van 'Het Lam Gods' retabel. Kritisch onderzocht*, s.l. (Maldegem), s.d. (1984).

Andrea De Kegel, *Het Lam Godsretabel door Jan en Hubrecht Van Eyck,* in: De Sint-Baafskathedraal van Gent. Een kunstkamer (ed. Geert Van Doorne), Openbaar Kunstbezit in Vlaanderen, 1992, 1.

Elisabeth Dhaenens, *Het retabel van het Lam Gods in de Sint-Baafskathedraal te Gent*, inventaris van het kunstpatrimonium van Oost-Vlaanderen, VI, Ghent, 1965.

Elisabeth Dhaenens, *Hubert en Jan Van Eyck*, Antwerp, Mercatorfonds, 1980.

Alfons L. Dierick, *Van Eyck. Het Lam Gods*, Ghent, 1972.

Fabrice Hadjadj, *L'Agneau Mystique. Le retable des frères Van Eyck*, Paris, Ed. de L'Œuvre, 2008.

Anne Hagopian Van Buren, *Van Eyck, art. in: The Dictionary of Art* (ed. J. Turner), Grove, 1996, pp. 703–715.

Karel Mortier, Noël Kerckhaert, *Dossier Lam Gods. Zoektocht naar De Rechtvaardige Rechters*, Ghent, 1994.

Peter Schmidt, *The Adoration of the Lamb*, Leuven, Davidsfonds, 2006.

J.R.J. Van Asperen-De Boer, *A Scientific Re-examination of the Ghent Altarpiece*, in: Oud Holland XCIII (1979), pp. 141–214.

Harold Van de Perre, *Van Eyck. Het Lam Gods*, Tielt, Lannoo, 1996.

Leo Van Puyvelde, *Het Lam Gods*, Brussels, 1946.

http://closertovaneyck.kikirpa.be/

Text
Peter Schmidt

Translation
Ted Alkins

Design and typesetting
quod. voor de vorm.

Production
Emiel Godefroit

Printing
DeckersSnoeck

Photo credits
Sint-Baafskathedraal Gent © Lukas Art in Flanders,
photos Hugo Maertens and Dominique Provost.
except
p. 6: Koninklijk Museum voor Schone Kunsten Antwerpen
© Lukas - Art in Flanders vzw, photo Hugo Maertens;
p. 10: Rijksmuseum Twenthe, Enschede;
p. 18: Jose Huedo;
pp. 24-25: © KIK-IRPA, Brussels.

Every effort has been made to trace copyright holders. If, however, you feel that you have inadvertently been overlooked, please contact the publisher.

All rights reserved. No part of this publication may be reproduced or transmitted, in any form or by any means, electronic or mechanical, including photocopy, recording or any other information storage and retrieval system without prior permission in writing from the publisher.

© 2001, 2014, Ludion, Antwerp
ISBN: 978-94-9181-908-7 – D/2014/6328/6

www.ludion.be